Grief: A Mama's Unwanted Journey

SHELLEY RAMSEY

WESTBOW
PRESS
A DIVISION OF THOMAS NELSON

Scripture quotations marked ESV are taken from The Holy Bible, English Standard Version Copyright © 2001 by Crossway Bibles, a division of Good News Publishers. Used by permission. All rights reserved.

Scripture quotations marked KJV are taken from the King James Version of the Bible.

Scripture quotations marked NASB are taken from the New American Standard Bible, Copyright © 1960, 1962, 1963, 1968, 1971, 1972, 1973, 1975, 1977, 1995 by The Lockman Foundation. Used by permission.

Scripture quotations marked NIV are taken from The Holy Bible, New International Version®, NIV® Copyright © 1973, 1978, 1984, 2011 by Biblica, Inc.® Used by permission of Zondervan. All rights reserved worldwide.

Scripture quotations marked NKJV are taken from New King James Version Copyright © 1982 by Thomas Nelson, Inc.

Scripture quotations marked NLT are taken from the Holy Bible, New Living Translation, copyright© 1996, 2004, 2007 by Tyndale House Foundation. Used by permission of Tyndale House Publishers Inc., Carol Stream, Illinois 60188. All rights reserved.

WestBow Press books may be ordered through booksellers or by contacting:
WestBow Press
A Division of Thomas Nelson
1663 Liberty Drive
Bloomington, IN 47403
www.westbowpress.com
1-(866) 928-1240

ISBN: 978-1-4908-0619-8 (sc)
ISBN: 978-1-4908-0618-1 (hc)
ISBN: 978-1-4908-0620-4 (e)

Library of Congress Control Number: 2013915307

Printed in the United States of America.

WestBow Press rev. date: 9/18/2013

Cover photos by Wyatt Ramsey.

for my men:
may you always know deep in your marrow the relentless love of Jesus

Contents

Foreword

I walked with Shelley and Phil as a friend prior to, during, and after Joseph's death and know them well. When Shelley told me she was thinking about writing a book about her experiences, I encouraged her. I knew hers was a compelling story. But when she asked me to proof the actual manuscript, my inclination was to refuse, knowing that I had not fully dealt with my own grief, sorrow, confusion, and anger arising from this terrible event—the death of my godson, Joseph. In spite of my trepidation, I agreed to read. After reading (and rereading) Shelley's manuscript, I can attest firsthand to the healing, hope, and restoration Shelley's words provide.

As a pastor for over two decades and having counseled many people dealing with grief, I highly recommend this book to anyone who has experienced the loss of a loved one, but especially to those who have lost a child.

—Rev. Rusty Webster, R.N., B.S. Ed., M.Div.

Introduction

Amidst all our hopes, dreams, and plans as parents, we never plan to bury a child. For a parent, it is the most unthinkable nightmare. If you're reading these pages, it is most likely because you have buried a child or someone you dearly love. Or perhaps you've come alongside a dear friend and are walking arm in arm down this horrible road named Grief. My heart, mind, and body ache for you.

Eleven years ago, my husband, Phil, and I buried our firstborn son, Joseph, who was only seventeen, and our sons Curt and Wyatt buried their older brother. We all continue to miss him each and every day. And despite my yearning not to, I have lived to tell of this loss and the many ways it has shaped my journey.

Although I don't know your specific circumstances, I know your spirit is wounded. My spirit groans with yours. I know your pain is deep. I know what it is to wish you were in that grave yourself. I know what it is to dread waking in the morning and to want to clobber the next person who tells you that you should move on with life. I get that there are times when all those words of comfort make your aching head explode and fail to heal your broken heart.

Please know that every thought, every page, and every word has been bathed in prayer for you specifically. I have prayed that your grief process would be expedited and have asked God in advance to comfort you and love you through these pages. Lean into Him and look for His grace as you travel this unwanted and painful journey.

I am immensely private but have opted to open this chapter of my life in hopes that it will help you find comfort in the midst of your suffering. I discovered things that helped me work through the grief and quickly learned what worked against it when dealing with the searing pain.

I am a woman of faith. I knew and loved the Lord before tasting death. Even so, there were times in the most intense moments of my grief that my faith was challenged and seemed so fragile. Many years later and on this side of grief, I finally have oneness with Him that I might otherwise never have known. And for that I am grateful.

I have arranged this book so you can quickly find the section your heart needs most at the moment. Some are entries from our personal journals. I share my experience so you will understand that you are not alone and are not going crazy. Each entry is very personal, and some of the content is difficult to digest. I think you will relate.

It's just the two of us now, you and me. One thing I've come to learn in my half century of life is that we all have a story. What follows is the most significant chapter in mine.

Prologue

Meet Joseph

Joseph is the first of my three great love stories. He was not perfect, but he was wonderful. He welcomed me into motherhood and introduced me to the delightful world of boys: catching lightning bugs, cowboys and Indians, and weird boy noises. He acquainted me with *Goosebumps* books, taught me how to build a fort with wooden blocks, and helped me appreciate the mad skills of GI Joe.

Before him, I knew nothing about shooting BB guns, the rules of baseball, or a roundhouse kick. Had I not given birth to him, my life would have been void of Duke basketball, *The Godfather Trilogy*, and Pepsi.

From my eldest, I learned discipline as I watched him work hard so he could pay cash for his car and one of life's greatest lessons in respect while witnessing my son's genuine interest in people from all walks of life. I was graced with watching God's plan unfold as Joseph's faith matured.

On February 23, 2002, Joseph was welcomed into heaven. He is home, and I am homesick.

CHAPTER

1

Our Lives Forever Changed

Let him rest,
Heaven blessed.
Bring him home.

—Les Misérables, "Bring Him Home"

On that mild February morning, my husband, Phil, stood at Joseph's bedroom door, hand raised, ready to knock. But then he thought, *No, he is seventeen. He can get himself up if he really wants to come with me.* So Phil waited to see if Joseph would tumble out of bed to join him for the men's breakfast at church that morning.

A normal Saturday morning at the Ramsey's meant a big breakfast—French toast, scrambled eggs, and bacon. The boys would get their chores underway while I cooked, and then we'd clean up together after breakfast. After that, everyone was free to enjoy the day. But this Saturday we weren't having a big family breakfast. We were scattering in different directions.

Curt, our middle son, would be off for the day with the youth group helping on a friend's farm. Our youngest, Wyatt, had planned to spend the day with Joseph but the night before was invited to the next round of a 4-H talent competition and was needed at tryouts that morning. He was performing a tae kwon do kata to music. Normally, I would have enjoyed a

relaxing day home from work, but I would be taking Wyatt to his tryouts—
an outing that annoyed me at the time.

Joseph was so excited to be accompanying his dad for his first men's
breakfast. Joseph's church life was always important to him as was spending
time with his dad. So he did indeed get up in time and shower. He even did
his chores the night before so they wouldn't go undone while he was out.

Joseph emerged from his room dressed and eager to join his dad. I still
remember exactly what he was wearing: jeans, long-sleeved T-shirt, navy
windbreaker with a white stripe across the chest, and new sneakers.

Phil and Joseph had a great time together at the men's breakfast,
sharing a table and enjoying bacon, eggs, and biscuits. Phil was laughing
and joking with the men as usual and noticed Joseph watching him with
that sheepish grin of his as if to say, "There goes my dad again." Phil
remembers Joseph looking at him every time he glanced his way.

After the gathering came to a close, the tables were cleared and
the room was put back in order. Joseph and his friend Aaron, who had
also attended the breakfast, prepared to leave. They were headed to an
electronics store thirty-five miles away to purchase a CD player for Joseph's
car. His dad and I had given him a gift certificate for Christmas to get one,
and Joseph had waited two months to make his purchase, researching the
best deal. That was our boy, frugal and responsible. Now he was finally
going to get that CD player. After a trip to the electronics store and lunch
at Burger King, the boys would head back to Aaron's family farm where
Aaron, who could fix anything, would install the CD player.

Phil and a few of the men were going to help a church member move.
As Joseph and Aaron were heading out the door, Joseph asked his friend
to wait so he could tell his dad good-bye. Those two men of mine hugged
one another. Phil's last words to his oldest son were, "I love you."

Joseph hopped into Aaron's car, and they made a quick stop by our
house to pick up Joseph's car. Their plan was to leave Joseph's car at a fire

station halfway between home and the electronics store and then ride the rest of the way together. Before heading out, Joseph ran into the house to tell me good-bye, but I wasn't home. Though my heart hurts that I missed that last good-bye, I take great comfort in knowing that we left nothing unfinished. No doubt he would have told me he loved me; we were just that way. I know he loved me, and he knew I loved him.

Joseph and Aaron had a good time that morning. They found the CD player Joseph wanted and enjoyed lunch together at Burger King. When Joseph paid for his lunch, he donated a dollar to support children with muscular dystrophy. A shamrock bearing his name was then taped to the wall there.

On the way home, the boys stopped at the fire station to pick up Joseph's car as planned so he could follow Aaron back to the farm. Aaron later told us that Joseph got into his car and then got back out and thanked him again for helping with the CD player. Those were the last words Joseph spoke to anyone. They never made it to the farm. Just shy of Aaron's driveway, Joseph wrecked his car.

Only three hours after breakfasting with his dad and the men of the church, Joseph's car lay demolished beneath a tree, his new CD player still in its box, his life on this earth over. And our lives on this earth forever changed.

CHAPTER

2

My Father Would Find Me and Call Out My Name

But none of it mattered after the game
When my father would find me
And call out my name
Dreaming of glory the next time out
My father showed me what love is about.

—Bob Bennett, "A Song about Baseball"

The men from church were still helping with the move when our dear friend and pastor, Dane, received a call that Joseph had been in an accident. He was standing with Phil on the porch at the time. After Dane hung up the phone, he looked directly at Phil and said, "Joseph has been in an accident." Dane tried to convince Phil to let the other men gather and pray before they left, but Phil only wanted to get to his boy as fast as he could.

God's mercy carried Phil that morning in his deepest anguish. It is clear to us that God handpicked Dane to be with Phil as the news of Joseph's accident unfolded. Phil was serving under Dane at church as an elder at that time. But even more importantly, Phil and Dane had been meeting together weekly for some time and had developed an intimate fellowship as well as a strong brotherly love for one another. I, too, had a close connection with Dane through our church body both in worshipping and in my role as the church administrator. Our lives were richly woven together in the only kind of strong fabric that can bear up under such grieving.

The twenty-mile drive across the county seemed to take forever. Phil was used to a Dane who loved speed and driving fast, but this ride crept along at a snail's pace. Everything seemed a blur. He did not look out the window. He struggled to keep himself from thinking too much, from fearing the possibilities. He felt trapped and suffocated, unable to do anything to help his son.

From Dane's cell phone, Phil called Carolyn, Aaron's mother. She was hysterical. Her words, although incomprehensible, expressed all the fears he couldn't bear to consider. The realization that Joseph might be seriously injured, even dead, bored its way into his mind. He hung up and called our close friend Bill. No answer. He left a message: "Bill, Joseph has been in a terrible accident. I am trying to find you and Linda. I don't know what to do. Will you please call me as soon as you can?"

As Dane and Phil turned down that narrow, winding country road, Dane gently warned Phil, "We're getting close." Beyond the state trooper and the flashing lights of fire trucks and police cars and an ambulance, about fifty yards in the distance they could make out the shape of Joseph's car. Phil threw open his door before the car came to a stop. With pounding heart, he sprinted down that country lane in search of his son.

The state trooper intercepted Phil, held up his hand, and commanded him to stop. "I'm his dad!" demanded my husband, grabbing the officer's chest. "Is he dead?" The trooper, unable to speak, nodded.

Phil saw his friend Jay, an EMT, standing in front of the ambulance, another one of God's mercies that day. Jay was pulling off his gloves and shaking his head. Next, Phil saw Joseph's car in the distance and glass shattered over the road. He tried to run to it but was held off and told there was too much broken glass. The weight of the truth landed on him with a thunderous crash, piercing pain, excruciating horror, and total awareness that he would not see Joseph again this side of heaven.

Overwhelmed, Phil's body shook with rage. He insisted to Jay that he be allowed to see Joseph. Dane and Jay were both acutely aware of Phil's strength as a black belt in that moment. He was determined to get past Jay, but Jay compassionately warned him, "You don't want to see him now, trust me on this. You can see him at the hospital."

Phil finally let go and surrendered to his friend, saying, "I trust you, Jay." Then collapsing to the pavement, he cried out, "Joseph, where are you?" And again "Joseph! Joseph, I love you more than I love myself. I love you more than life itself." Everyone at the scene was in tears.

It took all the strength Dane and Jay could muster to peel Phil off the pavement and raise him up. He thought he was suffocating. His vision was blurred. He was hyperventilating and in danger of fainting. Jay insisted that Phil breathe and try to relax his body. Jay and his wife, Anna, also an EMT, carried the inconsolable, grief-stricken father to Dane's car.

From the scene, Dane drove Phil to the hospital. Dane told me that ride was like a heavenly courtroom with Phil and God with Phil giving a lengthy telling of all of Joseph's virtues compared to Phil's sins and a complete bewilderment at the judgments of God. "How could He? How could He allow this injustice? How could He take innocent Joseph and leave guilty Phil? Why?" Phil pounded the dashboard, yelling, "Of all people, of all people, why Joseph?"

Chapter

3

Where You Are Meant to Be

May today there be peace within.
May you trust God that you are exactly
where you are meant to be.
May you not forget the infinite
possibilities that are born of faith.
May you use those gifts that you have received, and
pass on the love that has been given to you.
May you be content knowing you are a child of God.
Let this presence settle into your bones, and allow your
soul the freedom to sing, dance, praise, and love.
It is there for each and every one of us.

—Teresa of Ávila, *Prelude to Eternity*

I hate that I wasn't there. I was there for my son's very first breath. If he had to draw his last breath, I wanted to be with him then as well. But God had other plans.

I hate that I wasn't with Phil. The image of my grieving husband on that country road without me is painful. I am grateful to God for Dane's presence with him during the worst moments of his life.

And I am so grateful Wyatt was with me, safe. He had planned to accompany Joseph that day. But because I was off work and Wyatt was invited to the next round of a talent competition, his transportation became my responsibility. The thought of losing Wyatt too is unfathomable. At the time, I was annoyed at having to take him to tryouts, but it is now one of the things for which I am most grateful. I thank God every time I hear my youngest laugh, when I look at his latest piece of art, and when I bask in his enthusiasm as he shares with me the details of what is rolling around in his brilliant mind.

By noon, Wyatt and I had returned home, and he was readying for a group of boys to come play. I was cleaning out the refrigerator when the phone rang.

It was Dane's wife, Krista. She said, "Shelley, Joseph's been in an accident." I asked if he was okay, and she said she didn't know. I didn't even think to ask her how she knew about the accident; I just did what mothers do when their children get hurt. I purposed to find and take care of my son. I thanked her for calling and told her I'd head to the hospital. I didn't ask if Joseph was there, and Krista did not say. I just assumed that Joseph as a minor would need to be examined and that I needed to be with him. Krista asked if there was anything she could do. Knowing how long ER waits can be and that I might be gone awhile, I asked her to come over long enough to send Wyatt's friends home when they arrived. I didn't want a house full of sixth graders left unattended.

As I was trying to get out the door, my phone rang again. Hoping it was Joseph or Phil, I answered. But it was Aaron's mother, Carolyn. She was crying, saying how sorry she was. I could barely understand her but thought she was overreacting to a fender bender. I told her I needed to hang up and get to the hospital in the event Joseph needed treatment. The gravity of this day was just not sinking in.

When I arrived at the ER, I spoke with a lady at the desk. "I was notified that my son was in an accident. His name is Joseph Ramsey."

"Is this the accident on Route 683?" she inquired. I had no idea. She asked my name, took my insurance card, and escorted me into another room, saying I'd be able to see the ambulance arrive from there. At that moment, it all seemed routine to me.

I don't know how long I waited, but the longer I stayed, the more scenarios danced through my mind. At first, they were only of mild concern: maybe he'll need stitches; maybe he'll have a slight concussion. I knew Joseph would be so disappointed in himself for having an accident after signing up for a program with our insurance company to earn a one-thousand-dollar savings bond. All he had to do was stay incident-free his first three years of driving. He was always so careful and responsible, looking for ways to earn and save money.

The sanitary hospital smell was getting to me and my resulting headache agitated me. *Maybe he has just gone home, and I've been wasting time sitting here. I shouldn't have left Wyatt at home. I want him with me. I wonder when Curt will be home? I can't remember what he told me. I want to hear about his day. Good grief. What is taking so long? I have things to do, dinner to prepare for my men. I promised I'd make éclair cake for dessert, and I haven't even baked the pastry. What is taking so long?*

Eventually, a nurse came in. "Is there anyone I can call for you while you wait for the ambulance?" he asked.

I asked for my friend Karen. She had a comforting way about her and a calming voice. More importantly, she held an important position at the hospital and would find out what was taking so long. But no, she wasn't there. I asked for my friend Steve, the hospital pharmacist. No, Steve was not on duty. "That's okay," I said. "I'm fine." I had no idea.

As I endured the extended wait, it occurred to me that I was not in the general waiting area but instead was sitting in an ER staff lounge. Personnel wandered in and out and nodded, forced smiles on their faces. More scenarios raced through my mind. Possibilities were sinking in. *Maybe Joseph will require hospitalization. Or surgery. He might be badly burned. Or horribly maimed.* For a fleeting moment, I began to consider that Joseph might be dead. Finally, a doctor walked into the room. Relief.

"Mrs. Ramsey," he said flatly. "I'm Dr. Ramsey. I don't think we're related."

"I'm sure we're not," I said.

He continued. "Mrs. Ramsey, your son Joe was in an accident."

"Joseph," I corrected. "His name is Joseph."

"Well, Mrs. Ramsey, Joe died."

Numbness fell over me and then swiftly turned to anger. *Who is this stranger telling me my son is dead? Who does he think he is? Did he not hear me tell him my son's name? It wasn't a suggestion. It is his name!* I shut Dr. Ramsey out after that. He became an intruder. I remember nothing about what he looked like, nor do I know if he said anything else.

I cried out for Joseph. I wanted my men. Somebody, I don't know who, told me Phil was on his way. I just knew I needed Phil. I waited . . . and waited. I was there by myself, alone for what seemed an eternity.

Chapter

4

Wallet, Watch, and Tears

You will lose someone you can't live without, and your heart will be badly broken, and the bad news is that you never completely get over the loss of your beloved. But this is also the good news. They live forever in your broken heart that doesn't seal back up. And you come through. It's like having a broken leg that never heals perfectly—that still hurts when the weather gets cold, but you learn to dance with the limp.

—Anne Lamott, *Plan B: Further Thoughts on Faith*

Phil staggered into the hospital enveloped in a dark cloud of pain and tears. I knew the minute I saw him that it was true that our boy was dead. We held onto each other for dear life and sobbed . . . and sobbed . . . and sobbed. My heart felt like it was being ripped in two. I became ill and had to run to the bathroom. When I returned, I sat on the cold floor, and Dane wiped my brow with a wet paper towel. He, too, was in pain.

I was desperate to see my babies. True, they were in the sixth and ninth grades, but at that moment, each one was my baby, and I needed to embrace them both. I needed to smell their aliveness and feel their hearts beating. I needed to look at them, whole.

Friends picked up Curt and Wyatt and brought them to us. We asked they only be told that Joseph had been in an accident, and that we needed them to join us at the hospital. So many thoughts and feelings ran through my head and heart.

My mind darted to instant replays. I recalled Joseph making each of us laugh until we cried the previous Christmas Eve when he gifted his brother with a sandwich. I flashed back to the moment he was born and then to memories of my three boys making sand sculptures together on the beach. *How am I going to tell my boys their big brother is gone? How am I going to pull myself together enough to comfort them? I want to protect the innocence of their childhood. I want Joseph's childhood back.* Every thought made me violently ill.

My boys arrived. Never had they looked so beautiful. I don't remember which one arrived first. I just know I lunged for each one and held him tightly. With each of their entrances, Phil, in his tremendous anguish, blurted out, "Joseph's dead." The four of us held each other close. I didn't want to let go.

Soon thereafter, two state troopers walked into the room. Each politely removed his hat and then offered sympathy and assurance that our boy was not speeding and was wearing his seat belt. I had no doubt about either. Joseph was the most responsible person I knew.

So many irresponsible people live to an old age—drunk drivers, drug dealers, murderers, and abusive parents. Yet my loyal, reliable, and very mature son with a promising future was . . . dead. The irony is still lost upon me. God's plan remains a mystery.

One of the officers handed me a brown envelope marked "Valuables Envelope" that contained the contents of Joseph's pockets. The contents were listed one by one: "One Ten-Dollar Bill ($10.00), One Five-Dollar Bill ($5.00), Five One-Dollar Bills ($5.00), and One Timex Watch—Digital w/Plastic Band." It then read, "Total Cash $20.00. Nothing Follows." Nothing follows. There was nothing to follow. That was the end of my son.

Wyatt took the envelope from me and lovingly removed his brother's wallet. He put the wallet in his own back pocket after respectfully handing the money to me. I pulled out the watch I had purchased for Joseph for Christmas when he was eight years old. He had long outgrown it but didn't want a new one. He just carried it in his pocket. The alarm was set to wake my boy each morning at 7:30. It went off daily for months after that. We never turned it off.

Chapter

5

His Unique Perspective

Grief is not just a series of events, stages, or timelines. Our society places enormous pressure on us to get over loss, to get through grief. But how long do you grieve for a husband of fifty years, a teenager killed in a car accident, a four-year-old child: a year? Five years? Forever? The loss happens in time, in fact in a moment, but its aftermath lasts a lifetime.

—Elisabeth Kübler-Ross, *On Grief and Grieving*

Before we left the hospital, an employee asked if we would consider organ donation. Upon receiving his driver's license, Joseph had decided to become an organ donor. Phil and I wholeheartedly supported his decision, as we, too, are organ donors. Looking back, I wonder what allowed me to move through those decisions without an even deeper level of trauma. It must have been part shock and part my matter-of-fact personality. When I see something in my family that needs tending to, I tend to it. Whatever it was, I have never regretted our decision to donate all that was viable.

We were told his corneas could be donated. His beautiful green eyes. When Joseph was a teen, Phil had a conversation with him about his interest in filmmaking—all aspects of film, including acting. Phil explained to him that actors don't need to be gregarious extroverts. He pointed to Clint Eastwood, a very shy and private actor, whose compelling portrayals in film were accomplished with subtle movements, particularly of the eyes.

Joseph's eyes had a similar power, a similar depth. They were the still waters. Their dark warmth drew people in, and their gentle perspective held them there. His eyes revealed a subtle honesty and integrity that was almost intimidating.

Those eyes read voraciously. From the day he learned to read, Joseph was never without a book. Month after month, year after year, he spent his money on books.

Yes, we wanted to gift someone with Joseph's eyes, with his unique perspective.

We were also told that his skin could be shared. We learned that, after a long process, it would be used for burn victims, most notably survivors of the 9/11 attacks. Yes, Joseph would have wanted that. He would have liked helping innocent people, to be a part of all things working together for good for those who love God. Yes, use his skin and also his bones to help others. Give his death a life-giving purpose. Allow others to live more fully.

One month later, I received a letter from the eye bank that read, "Take comfort in knowing that both donated corneas were transplanted. Two people are now able to see a sunset, a mountain range, or a loved one's smile because of this difficult decision your family made." Likewise, I received a letter the following fall informing us of the many ways Joseph's bones and tissue had been distributed. It read:

To date, there have been ten life-enhancing grafts distributed for transplant from Joseph's donation.

Tendon grafts are used in orthopedic repair of congenital defects or injured shoulders, knees, and other areas of the body. There have been, to date, six such grafts distributed to hospitals for implants.

The gift of human bone typically results in the formation of numerous grafts that are used in various surgical procedures, generally in spinal fusion surgeries in the cervical and lumbar areas. Bone grafts are used commonly in orthopedics to facilitate healing of fractures and rebuilding or remodeling of bone for total hips and knees. There have been three distributions of such grafts as a result of your donation.

Cancellous bone is used in various forms of oral and maxillofacial repair. Cancellous bone has been distributed to one hospital for use.

Joseph's gifts improved the quality of life for many. Even in death, he was responsible and giving.

CHAPTER

6

Short Trip, Long Drive

The best moment of a Christian's life is his last one, because it is the one that is nearest heaven. And then it is that he begins to strike the keynote of the song which he shall sing to all eternity.

—C. H. Spurgeon, *Spurgeon's Gems*

I think it was a nurse who said we could not see Joseph's body until the next morning. I don't know why I didn't insist on seeing him immediately. The fact that I did not kiss that beautiful face his last day troubled me in the dark hours of the nights that followed. I was the first to kiss him when he arrived; I should have been the last to kiss him the day he left. I should have been the one to wipe the blood from his face, to prepare his body for burial. This is one of the things God and I have had to reconcile over time.

We left the hospital a family forever changed. Others offered to drive us home. I declined and drove us. We live less than a mile from the hospital, yet that short trip was the longest drive we've ever made. Not one of us uttered a single word. We drove home in complete silence. When we entered our home, we immediately formed a little circle and hugged one another and cried hard. Shortly thereafter, I went to my desk, picked up the phone, and called my sister. I gave her the grim task of contacting family for me, as I could not make that call more than once. Phil then called his brother and requested the same of him. Wyatt went straight to his oldest brother's room. He gathered Joseph's Bible and a few other sentimental items and took them to his own room. Curt went into his own bedroom and closed the door.

After calling my sister, I went upstairs and looked around my son's room. We gave him the smallest, knowing he'd be the first to move out. He was supposed to leave for college, not be put in the ground. I looked at his books. He loved to read; he was never without a book. A half-eaten pack of Reese's Pieces—sweet tooth, my boy; sports memorabilia—Dallas Cowboys, Duke Blue Devils, and Cleveland Indians; TV on the dresser—country music stations always blocked; tae kwon do black belt tossed over the closet rod and shoes in perfect alignment.

I pulled a dirty black sweatshirt from the laundry basket on his floor and tried to drink in his scent, to savor the essence of my sweet boy. There was no logo on the front, just a plain black sweatshirt. Unless it was one of his favorite teams, there was never a logo. He preferred his clothes plain and understated. It smelled like sweat and dirt. In his sweat, I could smell him. I inhaled it long and hard, wanting to permanently implant all of him in my brain, to make him last forever. The dirt bore the smell of his work ethic. He worked hard the day before, doing manual labor on a friend's farm. The thought of that made me smile. That boy of mine definitely preferred working with his brain to his brawn, but he had finished his senior year of high school at the end of the fall semester and was preparing to take some classes at our local community college to finish out the school year. In the meantime, he was willing to work anywhere he could to earn money for his future four-year-college tuition.

I heard the doorbell ring and gently placed the shirt back in the basket, knowing I'd return to it again. I did so several times over the next few days.

News of his death traveled quickly. Within hours, our home was overflowing with people we love.

CHAPTER

7

Anonymous Friends

The friend who can be silent with us in a moment of despair or confusion, who can stay with us in an hour of grief and bereavement, who can tolerate not knowing . . . not healing, not curing . . . that is a friend who cares.

—Henri Nouwen, *Out of Solitude*

The first to arrive at the house after the crash was Mr. Jackson and his wife, Linda. Mr. Jackson was Joseph's, Phil's, and Wyatt's tae kwon do instructor, and the Jacksons had become good friends of ours. Jay, who had also taken tae kwon do, had called and informed him of Joseph's death. Now this giant, athletic man was sitting on my couch, one leg outstretched and holding my husband's hand, tears streaming down his face as he listened to our anguish. He said nothing; he offered no words of wisdom or explanation as to why God had allowed this. It is hard to convey the comfort and security of having someone just hold your hand while you are grieving.

Linda noticed the salmon I had on the counter that I was going to grill that night for my men. So she fried it. Though my house reeked of fish for days, I loved her for doing that. Without asking what needed to be done, Linda did what she does best and made sure there was dinner for my boys.

Other friends came throughout the evening. They put clean sheets on our beds, brought in tables and chairs, and stocked the bathrooms.

Everything that was necessary for the family and friends who would soon gather in our home was taken care of. At that time, tending to such details would not have occurred to me, a normally meticulous, detail-oriented person.

As our home filled quickly with friends that evening, it became a bit overwhelming for Curt and Wyatt. So a family friend, Kevin, took them to play basketball at his house, offering solitude and release. I didn't want them to leave my sight, but I realized that was what they needed at that time.

Later in the evening, our friend Dave prayed for us. Many friends participated in that prayer. Love filled our home, and God was very present.

The lengths God went to love us in practical ways in the days and weeks that followed were immeasurable. Some of the time I was aware of what was being done, but most of the time I was not. I lovingly refer to those dear ones used by God as my anonymous friends. They knew how to *do* love. They stepped in and did what needed to be done without asking and without expecting or wanting as much as a "thank you" in return.

Food arrived daily for nearly three weeks. A cooler of ice was brought in each morning and evening while my house was overflowing with people. My laundry was mysteriously washed, dried, and folded. Paper products were brought in so dishes didn't need washing. Even the paper towel holder stayed full. Lunch was anonymously paid for at a Chinese restaurant. A pizza showed up another day for dinner. A basket of teas landed on the doorstep with a note reading, "Be good to yourselves." The deliverymen at Domino's Pizza donated an entire day's tips. Money given by family, church, and friends covered our son's funeral expenses.

Another very meaningful gesture was from Aaron. Even in his grief, he drove all the way back to Burger King, removed Joseph's shamrock from the wall, and brought it to us. On the back, he wrote:

Phil, Shelley, Curt, and Wyatt,

This shamrock is a symbol of Joseph's enormous heart. We both bought one when we stopped to eat in Danville. Even to the end, he was thinking of helping others. That was Joseph's way of showing his love for God to others. Every time you look at this, remember his love.

Aaron

What a thoughtful thing for that eighteen-year-old young man to do! That paper shamrock is one of my most prized possessions, as it represents who my son was. His signature on the front was the last thing he penned.

Our anonymous friends saw us at our worst—and still loved us. They loved us through our grief, tears, and rudeness.

Unfortunately, there was the occasional person who insisted on shifting the focus to him—or herself. Our son died on a Saturday. The following Saturday, four days after burying our son, my husband received a call from a distant relative asking if he mailed a thank-you note for the twenty-dollar check she sent, as none had been received. We truly appreciated her generosity. In fact, we were overwhelmed by everyone's generosity. But thank-you notes? So soon? Who came up with rules of etiquette for the bereaved?

As is customary, the funeral home gave us a guest register for our friends and family to sign. For us, the register felt like an awkward way of tallying who did what, like a measure of how much we were loved. We knew we were loved, and likewise, we love our friends deeply. Phil and I never looked at that register or counted casseroles. Instead, it went in the trash, and we wrote one heartfelt thank-you letter and mailed it to each of our friends and family members.

8

No Coincidences

Coincidence is God's way of remaining anonymous.

—Albert Einstein, *The World As I See It*

As friends gathered with us in our home the evening Joseph died, our friend Rob asked if we had heard a new song, "I Can Only Imagine,"[1] a joyous, heartfelt song about heaven. We hadn't heard it, so he played it for us. We loved it and asked our dear friend Jamie to sing it at the memorial service. He had already been learning it, so he agreed. What a great song.

For me, picking up the pieces also meant listening to Joseph's music in the weeks that followed. He was always burning music onto CDs. I listened to the last one he burned before his death. The very last song, one he thought worth capturing and knowing, was "I Can Only Imagine." Coincidence?

"I Can Only Imagine" by Mercy Me
I can only imagine
What my eyes will see
When Your Face
Is before me
I can only imagine

I can only imagine.

After everyone left that evening, Phil and I finally lay down in our bed, trying to comprehend the reality of our son's death. We barely slept and clung to each other all night.

CHAPTER

9

Taking Leave

For the child of God, death is not the end but merely the door into a higher and more exalted life of intimate contact with Christ. Death is but the dark valley opening out into an eternity of delight with God. It is not something to fear, but an experience through which one passes on the path to a more perfect life.

—W. Phillip Keller, *A Shepherd Looks at Psalm 23*

The next morning, we went to see our Joseph, just the four of us. Because it was private and personal to us, we would not allow anyone else to see his dead body.

I don't remember who showed us where to go when we arrived at the hospital. I don't even know which floor we were on. I have no idea if we went to the morgue, an adjoining room, or a completely different part of the hospital. I just know with every corner I turned, my stomach churned as I anticipated seeing my son's dead body. The reality was beginning to settle in. I remember a lady cautioning us as we approached the doorway to be prepared for the bruising.

We entered the room and saw our boy lying on the hard table, his head propped up by an odd sort of pillow. I was overcome by his lack of color. Joseph's very pale body was dressed in a green hospital gown and covers were pulled up to his chest, his arms tucked into the blankets.

There was a bit of dried blood in one of his ears. I found a cloth and wiped it away.

Wyatt immediately became ill and wanted to leave the room. I was torn. I wanted to comfort my baby boy, hurting to his core, yet I needed time to see and feel the deadness of Joseph. I needed to take leave of him. Our dear friends, Bill and Linda, were waiting outside, so I took Wyatt to them, trusting God to love and comfort him through them.

As we viewed the body of our lifeless son, Phil wept. He cradled his son, head to his left, feet to his right, eyes closed. This was the same position he held him ten years earlier when he lowered Joseph into baptism. He then pulled Joseph's hand out from under the covers, wanting to hold it one last time. Curt was overwhelmed as he witnessed his dad hug Joseph's lifeless body.

I pulled Joseph's gown back a bit and saw the purple bruise across his chest caused by the seat belt. There was also a tiny bruise on his cheek and a few small cuts on his face. I was expecting much worse and didn't understand why they wouldn't let us see him sooner. I slipped his other hand out from under the cover and looked at his long fingers. One was still wrapped with a Band-Aid that was placed on it a few days earlier. I kissed his face, so cold, so empty—so unlike the soft, warm, pink little baby I had given birth to. I stroked his hair.

I knew this was only a shell of Joseph, and that he was no longer present. I knew where he was, and I wanted to be happy for him. But the throbbing ache of seeing my boy, now lifeless, wouldn't let me. I wanted to shake life into Joseph, shake the softness, warmth, and color back into my sweet boy. But he just lay there, stiff, motionless, unable to speak . . . gone.

CHAPTER

10

A Bed for My Boy

Rest quietly
Rest in His loving arms, for
He is watching over you
Ever faithful, ever true.

—Becca Mizell, "Be Still and Know"

After viewing Joseph's body, we went to the funeral home. We had to choose a casket and make final arrangements for this boy so full of life just twenty-four hours earlier. Brides take an entire year to plan a wedding; we had less than a day to plan the final farewell for our beautiful son.

I had nine months to prepare for Joseph's birth. Phil and I carefully selected his name, and I prepared a nursery for him, complete with hand-sewn balloons adorning the walls. I even made the quilt for his crib myself. It had a bouquet of bright-colored balloons on it, and the border was red with little white polka dots. I was anything but a seamstress, but when I brought my baby home from the hospital, I wanted to welcome him with a bright, colorful, fun nursery. Love was sewn into every crooked stitch.

I read many books about how to raise and care for my little boy. I had anticipated his arrival with joy and hope. But I was completely unprepared for his death. There was no book telling me how to take leave of him. I wanted time to stop. I wanted to erase the past twenty-four hours like my boys used to erase their drawings on an Etch-A-Sketch. Just briskly shake them away. I did not want to be in a funeral home!

I walked around the room looking for a casket, a final bed for the body of my child. I thought back to the bunk beds I bought ten years earlier. Sturdy beds for rambunctious boys to play on, build forts on, enjoy sleepovers, and then take to college. Money was tight then. I earned every dollar selling baby things and an old stove. I selected the bedding with care, something Joseph could grow into and would keep him warm through college. And now here I was at a funeral home, having to choose my boy's deathbed. We were paying nearly ten times as much for a casket only to have the ground swallow it whole as it cradled our boy's lifeless body.

We finally chose one of the least expensive coffins. It wasn't fine furniture he'd get to carry into adulthood and then pass down to his children. He was not going to spend eternity in it.

We then went to a room to meet with the funeral director. Our family has always been one to talk about death, as it is not a topic we are uncomfortable with or afraid of, and our boys have always known our wishes. Phil and I also have all the legal documents: will, health care power of attorney, and living will. But one thing that I'd never given a thought to was writing an obituary for one of my sons.

Phil and I filled out the standard submission form and let the newspapers word things the way they wanted. Joseph changed our lives when he entered our world, and he changed our lives when he left it. We could not articulate the power of his life in a two-by six-inch obituary.

CHAPTER

11

Arms Wide Open

Death is not the end of the road; it is only a bend in the road. The road winds only through those paths through which Christ Himself has gone. This Travel Agent does not expect us to discover the trail for ourselves. Often we say that Christ will meet us on the other side. That is true, of course, but misleading. Let us never forget that He walks with us on this side of the curtain and then guides us through the opening. We will meet Him there, because we have met Him here.

—Erwin Lutzer, *The Vanishing Power of Death*

We'd been told that Joseph's little red demolished car was towed to a garage. At the site of the wreck, Phil noticed that the windows were gone and the doors were smashed in. He later discovered that the obliterated hood was indented in the shape of the tree it hit. Apparently, the car had flipped up and hit a second tree over the front seats, as the roof was crushed all the way in. A trip to the site a couple of weeks later confirmed what we'd been told. The broken tree still lay off to the side of the road.

Phil asked our friend Joey to retrieve our son's belongings from the car, particularly the tape in the tape deck. Phil knew Joseph always played music in his car and insisted we play whatever song Joseph was listening to when he died at the memorial service. I was wary. He was a teenage boy, and I'd heard some of his music.

Joseph preferred music with a little edge. At only seventeen, he understood life came with an edge; that nothing ever goes quite as expected. Therefore, he preferred music that spoke truth and contained a realistic perspective of the world. Real and true, with some edge.

Joey brought us the tape. It stopped in the middle of the song "Arms Wide Open"[1] by Creed. Some of the words to this song were timely, almost fitting. As I listened to it at the memorial service, I thought about Jesus escorting and welcoming Joseph into heaven with His arms wide open, not only ready to receive Joseph, but also knowing all along that February 23, 2002 would be the day (Job 14:5). Joseph's time was in God's hands (Psalm 31:15).

"Arms Wide Open" by Creed
Now everything has changed
I'll show you love
I'll show you everything
With arms wide open

12

To Honor Our Son's Memory

If you allow it, suffering can be the means by which God brings you His greatest blessings.

—Charles R. Swindoll, *Insights on John*

I woke around 4:00 the morning after Joseph died and felt as though I had been pushed to the borders of my faith. So I prayed, asking God to give me something positive to do in the wake of my son's death, something that would honor Christ. Quite selfishly, I also wanted a project to keep me busy. In an effort to make something meaningful come from our son's death, we started the Joseph Ramsey Scholarship Fund.

I asked those wanting to remember Joseph to consider donations to a scholarship fund in lieu of flowers. Joseph's goal was to graduate college debt-free, and I wanted to help others do the same. The scholarship would not be for the brightest, most popular, or best looking but rather for those whose faith and character were as solid as Joseph's.

Giving this scholarship and holding a silent auction to fund it was an essential part of grief recovery for me. But I also allowed the preparations to postpone much of my grief. In hindsight, I wish I had delayed the auction a year. Instead, I rushed it, wanting to hold the auction on Joseph's birthday in June.

People all over the country donated items to be auctioned. There were autographs, sports memorabilia, services, home-goods, and art. With the help of dozens of friends holding my hand every step of the way and going above and beyond the call of duty, the auction was enormously successful. Each item and service sold, raising thousands of dollars.

The scholarship helped several well-deserving young people pay for their college education.

CHAPTER

13

Precious Blood

Too many Christians feel that grief is wrong, that we're supposed to rejoice when a loved one goes to be with the Lord. While we can rejoice in their homegoing, we can also grieve our loss.

—Bruce Barton, *When Your Father Dies*

Amidst the company, chaos, and planning, Phil slipped out of the house for a while. I had done that a time or two myself. As much as we appreciated the support of our loved ones, there were moments when we just needed space to breathe, quiet to digest the insanity of our son's death, and privacy to lament.

Joseph was a lot like me, but he was especially close to his dad. The two had a strong bond, deep respect, and love for one another.

Phil had a compelling need to return to the vehicle where his son's earthly life ended. When he had arrived at the crash site, the EMTs had discouraged Phil from looking at the car due to the vast amount of blood. Did they not know how precious the blood of his son was to him? He wanted to see it; he *needed* to see it. Phil left the house and went alone to the garage where it had been towed.

Phil looked over every smashed-up, tree-dented inch of the caved-in hunk of metal. He ducked into one of the missing windows and saw pieces of Joseph's hair on the ceiling and touched them. There was a large, crimson pool of dried blood on the seat and more splattered over the top of the seat. With a breaking heart, the grieving dad kissed every drop of blood soaked into the seat. That is extraordinarily beautiful to me and so demonstrative of the love my husband has for our sons.

Phil thought about how precious the blood of the Father's Son was to Him, the beloved Son in whom He was well pleased. And Phil was overwhelmed that God gave up His Son willingly (John 3:16).

Phil, the more emotional one of us, did the things he needed to grieve and begin healing his heart. He began purging his grief immediately, right at the site of the wreck and was instantly devastated. He embraced his grief no matter who was in the house those first days and no matter what was going on. He was able to shut everything and everyone out. Those first three days our family and friends thought he was having a nervous breakdown. Twelve-year-old Wyatt was so troubled that he hid the kitchen knives, fearing his dad was suicidal. Phil was emotionally real and raw, and his actions were a crucial part of his mourning process! I wish my boys and I had been able to do the same instead of allowing our grief to ferment.

14

Buried on Hallowed Ground

As I go into a cemetery, I like to think of the time when the dead shall rise from their graves. Thank God, our friends are not buried; they are only sown!

—D. L. Moody, *The D. L. Moody Book*

We asked our friend Bill to take Wyatt to select a burial plot. Whichever one he chose would be the one we would purchase. Wyatt selected one that was rows away from others because in his little boy mind "Joseph would not want to be around a lot of people." He also chose a gravesite next to the road so he'd always remember where it was. Wyatt loved his brother deeply and knew him well. And that love was reciprocated.

I pull the deed for Joseph's gravesite out of my files every now and then. We own that small piece of land. It was bought and paid for with our hard-earned money. But something is terribly wrong! Young parents shouldn't own a burial plot for a child. Nothing is more unnatural. My boys were supposed to bury me.

Until the resurrection, Joseph will only return in memories. He is buried on hallowed ground (1 Thessalonians 4:16). At the very place where we shed the most tears, we will have the most joy on Earth as that is the very spot from which his physical body will be raised. Nicholas Wolterstorff described it well. "Under each of these plots has been laid to rest what remained of one of God's images on earth, one of His icons. Those icon-remains hallow this place."[1]

I don't visit Joseph's grave as often as I used to, but when I do, I touch each letter of his name. Phil and I spent months selecting the name *Joseph Cole* for our firstborn. Now few speak it, so I go to the cemetery to see it written. The engraved lettering is understated—just plain, strong letters like the plain, strong, young man they represent. He is not there—and I long for heaven.

Chapter

15

Tucking Him In One Last Time

My heart was broken and my head was just barely inhabitable.

—Anne Lamott, *Traveling Mercies*

Phil and I chose to have a quiet, private graveside service for Joseph followed by a public memorial service later that evening. I wanted the graveside service to be very intimate, a time for my men and me to privately take leave of Joseph.

We woke that Tuesday morning, the day we would lay our son's body to rest. I showered, put on a little makeup, brushed my hair, and headed for my closet to find something to wear. I stood there, staring at my clothes. *What does a mama wear to her son's funeral?* I looked over my wardrobe. There were outfits purchased for work, church, and casual weekends but nothing to wear to the burial of my seventeen-year-old son.

I pulled out a dress and put it back, held up a pair of slacks and put them back too. I glanced at my comfy zip-up robe hanging on the hook and wanted to put it on, crawl into bed, and cancel the day. *This isn't normal! I don't want to do this! Maybe if I don't dress or show up, this won't be real.*

Phil walked into our room to ready himself to go. I asked him what I should wear, but that was the furthest thing from his mind. I grabbed a black skirt and a sweater and threw them on.

I walked down the stairs and discovered that my home had again filled with people. I loved them each and every one, but I wanted them to go away. *They can't all be here for the funeral. We very purposefully said it was private. We never announced the time or place. Who told them when it was? I can't deal with this. I need time and space for my men and me to say good-bye.* When we drove to the cemetery, each of them followed us there.

We stepped out of our van and onto the gravel drive leading up to a small handful of people dressed in black and our boy's dark-gray coffin. There was a slight drizzle, and the trees in the distance shook. As the body of our firstborn lay in the closed coffin, Dane began the service. "We gather this morning to say good-bye to Joseph."

Phil wailed, "Good-bye, Joseph." I wanted to comfort him, but I felt numb, paralyzed. I sat next to him, quiet and reserved on the outside yet torn to shreds on the inside. My mom sat next to me with Curt and Wyatt on her other side. I couldn't stand being separated from my boys and wanted to stop the service and rearrange the seating.

I wouldn't let myself cry. *Why am I trying so hard to hold it together? Is it because Phil is the only person here I'm that comfortable with?* I found myself practicing deep-breathing exercises, trying to hold it all in. I glanced over at the artificial grass rug covering the hole my son would soon be lowered into; I wanted to dive in, headfirst. I would have given anything to trade places with my son. I feared I was going to throw up again and thought how appropriate that hole would be to do so, the hole that now separated Joseph and me. The grief and nausea were so overpowering that I don't remember what else was said or whether or not we even sang a song.

When the service concluded, I stood up and covered my boy's casket with his baby blanket. The wind was blowing a bit, and I struggled to get it to neatly cover my baby's coffin. I know it made no difference to him, but I desperately needed to express my love for Joseph by tucking him in one last time. I gave him that light-green blanket the day he was born.

It was his first friend, and it comforted him and made him feel secure. Something in me was hoping to find comfort in that blanket myself that day. But I found none.

As we prepared to leave, Phil threw himself across the casket and cried. Once he gathered himself, he leaned over and hugged Curt who was standing next to him. As he glanced over his middle son's shoulder, the sun peaked through the clouds, and the grieving father experienced a sense of calm, the presence of God. The realization that Joseph, a strong believer in Christ, was alive in heaven brought Phil a sense of peace and security. He was by no means over his grief, but that was a crucial turning point for him.

The four of us went home after the funeral. I went upstairs and grabbed the black sweatshirt from Joseph's laundry basket and went to my room. I buried my face in it and tried to drink in the scent of him again. I then sprawled out on my bed, buried my head in my pillow, and hit the bed with my fist. I wanted to scream at the top of my lungs and cry until it no longer hurt. I wish I would have. Instead, I stuffed the pain down, trying to stay strong.

CHAPTER

16

He Is Home

Suffering, failure, loneliness, sorrow, discouragement, and death will be part of your journey, but the Kingdom of God will conquer all these horrors.

—Brennan Manning, *The Ragamuffin Gospel*

It was important to us that the emphasis be on Joseph's memorial service. Everyone was invited to attend. It was to be a celebration of Joseph's home-going, a time to a time to close our son's eyes in death, and open the eyes of the living. My family and I needed to break from our grief to worship and celebrate that Joseph was now face-to-face with Jesus Christ. We also wanted to convey Joseph's strong faith to those in attendance as an offer of hope. In the presence of death Jesus is the giver life.

I was expecting a small gathering of people, as Joseph was not a popular student, so I was overwhelmed when I entered the sanctuary and saw the large number of people. There were not enough seats. People had to sit in the choir loft and stand in the back. The sanctuary was full of family, friends, and people we barely knew. But what overwhelmed and touched me the most was the number of students. Friends of all three of my boys lined pew after pew.

Phil and I had asked three very dear friends to speak, men who had touched our lives and the life of our son in unique ways. Jim, our former pastor and one of Phil's dearest friends, spoke as did Rusty, my boys' godfather, also our best friend from Tennessee. Dane, who had been with Phil the morning of Joseph's death and who was our pastor, spoke and officiated. The Wednesday before he died, Joseph had just finished a Bible study led by Dane. During the course, the students were asked to write out their personal testimony. Dane read Joseph's testimony during the service.

The most memorable speaker, however, was Phil. He spoke with such clarity, fervency, and power that evening. I was amazed how, in all his grief and anguish and with all the people flowing in and out of our home, he had managed to get alone with his thoughts to pen what he would say. It was clearly God at work. Some of his words follow:

> Shelley and I are experiencing the deepest pain that can possibly be felt—it is a pain that will not go away. Curt and Wyatt are lost without Joseph. My boys were a trio; they were inseparable.

> I want you to understand how much I loved my Joseph. When he was little, I called him my buddy—and he still is. The pain I have is so great that the very thought of trying to live on right now is unbearable. Oh, I know I'll see Joseph in heaven—and you have no idea how badly I want to see him there right now—the sooner the better. Living seems ridiculous to me, but Joseph wouldn't want that. He wouldn't want me to "go off the deep end" or end my life or to "lose it." That would be dishonoring to him, and I want to honor Joseph because it was an honor to know him and to be his father.

> Only a few of you really knew our Joseph because, like his mama, he was a very private person. With family,

46

however, and especially with me, he was anything but private.

Joseph and I had a multitude, and I mean a multitude, of conversations. Most of the time, we discussed deep spiritual matters, our relationships with Christ, how to display grace to other people, hopes and dreams, why we do what we do, and issues around the world and how they affect us personally.

Joseph had many deep and sometimes disturbing questions. For you see, Joseph was very quiet and solemn and most of the time carried a sad note with him. He loved the color black and liked dark, dreary, cloudy days with stormy winds. In other words, he was very Christlike. Isaiah describes Jesus as a man of sorrows, acquainted with grief.

Joseph cannot speak to this community now, so to honor my Joseph and based on the countless conversations I had with him, I know exactly what he would want communicated to you. I prayed all day to be told what I should say. Therefore, these are Joseph's words, not mine. I agree with him—but these are his words! Remember that Joseph never took the popular route—he never licked his finger and held it up in the air to see which way the wind was blowing before he expressed his opinion.

The first thing Joseph would say is "Stop hating each other!" One of the things Joseph abhorred the most were people mistreating other people because they are different—which includes racial prejudice. This needs to stop!

Joseph loved sports and served as an umpire for a couple of years. He experienced firsthand the brunt and the fury of parents and coaches. A coach would be screaming in his face about a call, and Joseph would stoically wait until he finished and quietly but simply repeat his call. He would say to the leaders, coaches, and parents who should be building up and encouraging young people, "Grow up and act like adults!"

In many of our conversations, I revealed many of my own faults, weaknesses, and failures. And believe me, I have more than most have in three lifetimes. You see, Joseph hated hypocrisy in the worst way. He learned the lesson of the undeserved grace of God all throughout our relationship. He received and believed in unconditional love from God and also from me. No matter what Joseph, Curt, or Wyatt have done or will ever do—no matter what—I will always love them just the same. They will always be aware of and receive my enormous unconditional love just as I have from my heavenly Father. Therefore, Joseph would say to you, "Do not act like you have it all together in a clean-cut, rehearsed front to your children or anyone else. Why? Because you don't have it all together! Your children need to see the real you—flaws and all. If you believe in the forgiveness of God—take the mask off!"

Joseph also had a heart for the outcast, the downtrodden, the underdog, and those people who no one wanted to associate with. He genuinely cared about those who were lonely. He would say to you, "Please reach out to those in a personal way—one on one—and then do not advertise your good deed to everyone else when you do."

Tonight, Joseph receives his honorary second-degree black belt. I remember he was one of the men whom I had to fight when I earned my black belt. I was never so exhausted! After the last part of the test when I had to fight two men at once, I collapsed to the floor. Looking up, I saw the room spinning and fading out. In a couple of seconds, I regained my vision and immediately saw the face of my Joseph standing over me, hands on my shoulders, saying, "Dad, you made it! You made it!" The first thing I want to see when I die and reach heaven, which I hope and pray will be very soon, is my Joseph's face saying, "Dad, you made it! You made it!"

One more thing for those of you who have children still in the home: Do not let your child walk out the door unless you've given him or her a hug. Always do this, for you do not know if you will see him or her again.

Good-bye, Joseph. Good-bye, Buddy. It was an honor to be your father. I could live a thousand lives and never measure up to your stature. I love you and am proud of you immeasurably and beyond all comprehension.

—Dad

CHAPTER

17

Comrades

There never has been nor will there ever be, anything quite as special as the love between a mother and her son.

—Author Unknown, *What a Son Needs from His Mom*

When I buried Joseph, I buried my comrade. Like me, he was a firstborn, and our personalities were very similar. We were both introverted, private, comfortable with silence, and discerning. We were the organized ones of our home, my boy and I. Phil, Curt, and Wyatt are all artists. I joke that Joseph and I never had that problem.

Joseph's first breath took mine away. He stole my heart the second he was born. When he was handed to me, I inhaled him deeply into my heart, lungs, and mind. And God's purest form of love overflowed for my son. I knew he was on loan to me, and I was honored to be the one chosen to raise him. Raising my three boys was the reason I welcomed each morning. My heart broke the day God asked for Joseph back. I knew to hold him loosely, as I knew he didn't belong to me. But I never expected to bury him.

Those first few days after Joseph's death, I worked hard to hold it together, to make sure arrangements were made and my family was taken care of. By design and due to life's circumstances, I am a very strong and organized woman. I get things done. I'm just wired that way. Joseph was like that too. He wasted no time talking about what needed to be done. He just forged ahead.

Someone once asked me when Phil was going to let me have my turn, implying I didn't cry because my husband was grieving so badly. It upset me that someone would come into Phil's home and insult him, and it disappointed me that this person didn't realize that this is not who I am. So I continued taking care of arrangements and my family, albeit rather poorly, and grieved only in private or when Phil and I were alone. Some complimented my strength and ability to take care of things, saying I was full of grace. But I wasn't! I was in shock, doing all I knew to do—and waiting for everyone to leave.

Those first days when friends trickled by daily, I did fairly well. I knew people would be dropping by, especially around the lunch hour. Food was plentiful, and that seemed to be the time we had the most visitors. Lest it be mistaken as an invitation to enter my grief, I was up, showered, and had makeup on before anyone came to visit. That lasted about a week and a half.

Chapter

18

Cause of Death

Our death is just as meticulously planned as the death of Christ. There is no combination of evil men, disease, or accident that can kill us as long as God still has work for us to do. To those who walk with faith in God's providence, they die according to God's timetable . . . The immediate cause of death might be any number of things, but the ultimate cause is God. Yes, wicked men nailed Christ to the cross, yet we read, "But the Lord was pleased to crush Him, putting Him to grief" (Isaiah 53:10).

—Erwin Lutzer, *One Minute after You Die*

In the weeks that followed, Phil and I wanted to know as many of the facts about the wreck as we could. We firmly believe that February 23, 2002 was the day God intended to take Joseph home and therefore do not refer to it as an accident. But we wanted to know more about how he departed. We didn't want to go on the assumptions and speculations of the many who visited the site. We, too, had been there several times. We saw the skid marks and the broken cedar tree. But we wanted to hear what the EMTs and state troopers, those who had training to evaluate such things, had to say. We also had the accounts of Aaron and his family who were there.

The wreck occurred less than one hundred yards from Aaron's driveway. Joseph was following Aaron, not even driving fifty miles per hour. Knowing that Joseph was unfamiliar with that winding road, Aaron tapped his brakes to alert Joseph of the sharp curves. But despite Aaron's thoughtful warnings, Joseph wrecked. This was yet further confirmation of our belief that it was simply, albeit painfully, Joseph's time to go home.

Aaron witnessed the wreck in his rearview mirror, raced up the drive, and ran into his house screaming for his family to call 911, all the while fearing Joseph was already dead. Aaron and his family then ran down to be with Joseph until the EMTs and police arrived. Aaron and each of his family members noted that it was obvious that Joseph was already gone.

There are no words powerful enough to describe how humbly and utterly grateful we are that Aaron was safe and that he and his family stayed with our son until the EMTs arrived. I have no doubt that God hand-selected each of them to usher my boy into heaven. My prayer for them is that they will never forget how mightily God used them that day and that Jesus will be a constant source of comfort to each of them.

Within weeks of the wreck, we invited Jay, the EMT, to our home and asked him to share every detail. In preparation for this book, I again invited Jay and Anna for further discussion and confirmation of the accuracy of my description. Likewise, I asked Aaron and his family to share the details of that day, and each graciously wrote out his or her account.

The Jaws of Life was used on Joseph's vehicle before Jay was able to pull him from the shattered back window. Learning that Joseph died instantly and didn't suffer was comforting. Jay told us that when he arrived at the scene, Joseph's eyes were open, a sign that he had died instantly, and that he had no pulse or blood pressure. However, Jay let us know that, as the law requires, he did try to resuscitate him. But with each compression of his heart, blood squirted out his ears and brain matter out each canal.

The state troopers made a point to confirm what we already knew. Joseph was not speeding, nor were drugs or alcohol involved, and he was wearing a seat belt. As one officer assured us, "He did nothing wrong."

My boy, unfamiliar with that narrow, winding, country road, veered off the right side, overcorrected, and swerved to the other side. His car spun around and hit the ditch, causing the car to flip on its side. The top of the car hit the cedar trees, and the roof caved in. The result was that my firstborn died instantly from head trauma.

Phil and I ordered a copy of the medical examiner's report. The cause of death was confirmed.

CHAPTER

19

He Fixed His Eyes

So we fix our eyes not on what is seen, but on what is unseen, since what is seen is temporary, but what is unseen is eternal.

—2 Corinthians 4:18 NIV

Our twentieth wedding anniversary arrived one month after Joseph's death on a Wednesday. Big, expensive celebrations have never been our style but were even less so that year. Phil and I took the day off work so we could be together. It was a good time to find a stone for our son's grave. The ground had been too wet and soft for the cemetery to erect a headstone, and the grass had not grown back since the burial. But we weren't really ready before then either.

The memorial place was only minutes from our home. Granite or marble, flat or standing, round or rectangular . . . too many choices. That day was overcast and a bit breezy. We walked around outside looking at many stones, knowing we didn't want anything large or ornate. Joseph was created in the image of God, and the size and cost of the stone wouldn't change that. We chose a small, slightly masculine, dark-gray slab, one that would work on his downward-sloping grave. We found the owner to help us with our purchase.

"What would you like inscribed?" she asked. We tossed a few ideas around. Not once did we consider his GPA, his SATs, or his IQ. We didn't have written, "He remembered to say 'Yes, ma'am' and 'No, ma'am.'" You won't see "His room was always clean," "He was a black belt in tae kwon do," or "He was smart." When raising our three boys, all those things were important. Phil and I spent a great deal of time and effort teaching and training our boys. However, when Joseph's life ended so abruptly, the only thing that mattered was that our boy knew and loved Jesus Christ. He was a child of God. He was not a fan of Jesus, he was a follower. He lived his faith. So we wanted something befitting that. We wanted his testimony to be visible to passersby. Phil mentioned a verse in 2 Corinthians. Perfect. He grabbed a Gideon Bible to read it again, and I chose to make it personal.

Our boy's gravestone reads, "He fixed his eyes not on what was seen but on what was unseen."

CHAPTER

20

The Club Nobody Wants to Join

When a husband loses his wife, they call him a widower.
When a wife loses her husband, they call her a widow. And
when somebody's parents die, they call them an orphan.
But there is no name for a parent, a grieving mother or
a devastated father, who has lost their child. Because the
pain behind the loss is so immeasurable and unbearable that
it cannot be described in a single word. It just cannot be
described.

—Bhavya Kaushik, *The Other Side of the Bed*

Each of the cards, notes, and e-mails that arrived following Joseph's home-
going was cherished, but a few touched us deep down to where our souls
bled. Many of those came from complete strangers, other parents walking
this unwanted journey. I learned quickly that we had become a community
in and of ourselves. They got it. They, too, had been stung by death, had
buried a child. We are the club nobody wants to join, a club that prefers
no new members.

There are no barriers in this club. Race, religion, education, and
financial status do not matter. We've each experienced death; we've buried
the most precious part of ourselves, and our hearts throb.

My new friends assured me it was indeed normal for me to weave in
and out of the stages of grief, and that God could handle each emotion, no

matter how ugly. They assured me I wasn't losing my mind. They hugged me no matter what I did or didn't say.

Since Joseph's death, Phil and I have met dozens of other parents who have buried children either from lingering illness or sudden death. Some have horrific stories: children who were murdered, children who committed suicide, and circumstances that now involve costly lawsuits and families torn apart. Some have lost more than one child. But despite differing circumstances, there is a common thread that knits us together. We've each buried a child, and we each ache to the core of our existence. We feel as though a knife has been thrust into our gut that is permanently stuck.

A few parents were bitter, believing God did this *to* them. I found it best to spend little time with them while I was in the early stages of grief.

I asked my new friends questions others could not answer. How do I get through his birthday? The anniversary of his death? Mother's Day? What about his room? How do I get people to understand that I still have *three* sons? Will I ever stop wanting to die?

Phil and I attended Compassionate Friends, a support group for parents who have buried children, once a month for three months. Although heart-wrenching, it was cathartic meeting with others walking this unwanted journey. Each parent shared his or her story. We listened. We cried. We prayed for one another. Each of us was fragile and vulnerable, yet somehow strengthened by our connections to one another.

CHAPTER
21

A Family of Five,
a Table for Four

It's the neverness that's so painful. Never again to be here with us—never to sit with us at the table . . . All the rest of our lives we must live without him. Only our death can stop the pain of his death.

—Nicholas Wolterstorff, *Lament for a Son*

We received an e-mail from our friend Jamie days after Joseph died. His words resonated within me. "Aside from the grief, this can be hard on a marriage and family. Please give each other an extra measure of grace and a little extra attention." Phil and I respected our friend and heeded his advice as best we knew how and were able. We were determined to keep our family intact.

The loss of a child affects each family member individually as well as the family as a whole. It took time and effort for each of us to get used to Joseph's absence. Abundant grace was needed in the form of compromise and understanding. Our efforts were far from perfect, but we did the best we knew at the time. Phil, Curt, Wyatt, and I had to find a way to redefine our family, and we had to work through heavy fog to get there. It was not an easy, short, or pretty process.

When Joseph died, we each lost a different person, as we each had a unique relationship with him. Additionally, we have diverse personalities and varying needs. Our stories are different. If we each authored this book, the perspectives would vary widely.

We will always be a family of five. We never intended nor wanted to be a family of four, though we must now live as such. We feel a gap, a missing piece that will not be recovered. When dining out, requesting a table for four underscores that feeling.

In the months and years that followed, each of us had opinions as to what should or shouldn't be done with Joseph's room, clothes, and personal belongings. We had varying feelings as to how he should or shouldn't be remembered. We tried to respect one another's needs.

Phil would have kept Joseph's room the same indefinitely. But I was home much of the time and found it extraordinarily difficult to see it looking as though it were waiting for his return. After several months, we turned it into a computer room but left many of his things on the walls as Phil needed. As our needs have changed, it has been altered several times over the years. It was not a matter of right or wrong; it was respecting the needs of each family member.

For many years, we didn't take family pictures. This wasn't a deliberate decision. It was just difficult to capture celebrations or the ordinariness of life with a hole in the middle. It helps that we now have a precious daughter-in-law to include in our family photos.

Just days after Joseph died, we sat down to eat dinner at the dining room table. We each sat there, choking down our food, tears streaming down our faces, and no one speaking. There was no one in his chair; his side of the table had a gaping hole. A large part of the nightly conversation was missing. Everything felt wrong.

When Joseph was alive, dinner around the table was our time to discuss the day's events. It's where we *did* family. Sometimes we shared things we'd been reading. We laughed. We were a family of five. When he was little, Wyatt used to say, "Time for us to get a family conversation together." We loved that time of the day. But for the first year and a half after Joseph's death, we could not eat at that table. Truth be told, had it not been for fast-food drive-throughs, my men may have starved.

Eventually, Curt expressed missing eating together at the table. So we changed the room and tried again. We painted the walls a different color and bought a new rug and a new table and chairs. We hung different art. We didn't eat there every night, but we did eat there more often.

Prior to Joseph's death, we were very traditional in the ways we celebrated. Now, we didn't know how to fill that gap among us. Learning how to do that was a process. We discovered quickly that we each needed something familiar because life had become so unfamiliar. As they were part of the fabric of our family, we chose to hang onto many of our traditions.

The school year ended. I had a tradition of making the boys banana splits for breakfast to celebrate the last day of school. We were not going to get to celebrate high school graduation with Joseph, but Curt and Wyatt deserved to celebrate. Just surviving those horrendous three and a half months was cause for celebration. I got up that morning and made banana splits, and we carried on as best as we were able. Each scoop of ice cream was topped with hot fudge and drizzled with a few tears, but we pressed on.

The first holidays were extraordinarily difficult. Each of us around the table felt as though we had a limb missing. Joseph's absence was conspicuous, and his participation in our celebrations painfully nonexistent. We knew the date each holiday would arrive but had no clue how to celebrate without him. As each holiday rolled around, it felt as if the same limb had been ripped off again and again. Still, we gave thanks. With practice over the years, it became more natural.

Our best friends from Tennessee visit almost every Thanksgiving, and they came that first year. As we gather around the table, it is our practice to share what we're thankful for. That year, each of us mentioned something about Joseph. When Phil prayed before our meal, he again thanked God for the years we had with Joseph. There were other things to be thankful for as well: two healthy boys, jobs, family and friends, and our eternal hope. We were growing to understand that even in the midst of grief we can always find something to be thankful for.

CHAPTER

22

Make or Break a Marriage

The marriage relationship is one of God's creations for building up people. It gives husbands and wives the chance to minister to a mortal human being in a uniquely intimate fashion. To enjoy the meaningfulness of marriage, then, requires a once-made but ongoing commitment of mutual ministry to our mates, and the more we seize them, the more meaning our marriage will have.

—Larry Crabb, *The Marriage Builder*

Many marriages do not survive the death of a child. The more severe the grief, the more apathetic one may become. It's very easy to close yourself off from everyone, including the one who knows you best and loves you most. Phil and I saw that happen to others and purposed to prevent it from happening to us. We weren't exactly sure what to do or not do, but we committed to check in with one another and support each other in our different needs. It was as if we had made an unspoken vow that Joseph's death would not tear us apart. The result was that our friendship deepened to a level we hadn't known, one that couples achieve only after facing adversity of this magnitude.

Phil and I had a profound need to be together after our son died and did everything together that we possibly could. If we needed milk and bread, we both went to the store. This practice was a great comfort to us both.

Over time, our son's death strengthened our faith, and thus our priorities changed. I think we both became better people and better spouses to each other.

After thirty-one years and the death of a son, our marriage is healthier than ever. But Phil and I are no more special than anyone else. I am confident that we were being prayed for.

CHAPTER

23

A Kiss and a Charlie Brown Band-Aid

Children don't stop dancing
Believe you can fly
Away . . . away

—Creed, "Don't Stop Dancing"

No doubt the death of Joseph is the most painful thing I've ever experienced. A very close second was watching Curt and Wyatt grieve, knowing I could do nothing to take away their pain. I didn't want them to experience grief any more than I wanted Joseph dead. I wanted them to have their brother back. All this nearly destroyed me. I longed for the days I could fix everything for my boys with a kiss and a Charlie Brown Band-Aid. I wanted to pick them up and "kiss it all better" like I did when they were little.

Phil and I love each of our boys immeasurably. Joseph is not more special or more loved than his brothers, but rather he is different in that he has a grave. There is a void, and that void exists for his brothers as well. Their very happy childhoods were turned upside down the minute their brother died. Even a decade later, their brother's absence is painfully obvious, as each has realized that his wife will be absent a brother-in-law and their children an uncle.

After burying our eldest, it would have been easy to be overprotective of Curt and Wyatt. We fought that good fight, but admittedly, we were on edge every time they left our sight. They had earlier curfews than most of their friends. Forgetting to call to let us know they arrived at their destination safely was the unpardonable sin. We knew we were transferring our grief onto them and that they were bearing the burden of our anxiety, but Phil and I were incapable of reacting any differently.

I am intentionally saying little about how Curt and Wyatt handled the death of their brother and their consequent grief. They are now grown men and their stories are theirs to tell.

I would, however, like to encourage you, friend. As a mama, I was lost as to how to guide my sons through their grief, as I was drowning in my own. I loved them with every fiber of my being but was in uncharted territory. My sons battled grief and adolescence at the same time, a volatile combination. Concerned, I consulted a school counselor who asked if my boys understood the stages of grief. I didn't understand them myself and certainly didn't have the ability to explain them to my grieving sons. So consider professional grief counseling as a priority for each family member as needed. I didn't do this and wish I had. I wish I had started with myself.

Now on this side of grief, I can offer you suggestions for dealing with your surviving children. Keep them talking. Talk about their deceased sibling. Ask them about their favorite memories and their least favorite memories. Ask them how their grief is affecting them. Ask them if they're angry. If they are, together format a plan to deal with it. When the family is gathered together, ask specific questions: What would each of you like to do with your brother's (sister's) room? Is there anything that belonged to him (her) that is really special to you that you would like to have? Do you dream about your brother (sister)? Do you want to change any of our family traditions, and what is important to you to keep the same? Would you like to go with me to the cemetery today, or would you prefer to stay home? Please keep the dialogue open.

Pray with and for your children. Never let them forget how very much their heavenly Father loves them and that He has a plan for them.

Understand that Christ is your only source of genuine healing. Keep Him in the forefront of your life and your grief. His Word, your prayers, and the people He places in your life will work together to bring you through your grief.

CHAPTER

24

Grief Didn't Come
with Instructions

Why are the photographs of him as a little boy so incredibly hard to look at? Something is over. Now instead of those shiny moments being things we can share together in delighted memories, I, the survivor, have to bear them alone. So it is with all the memories of him. They all lead into blackness. All I can do is remember him, I cannot experience him. Nothing new can happen between us.

—Nicholas Wolterstorff, *Lament for a Son*

Many of the days, weeks, and months following Joseph's death were horrific. I grieved him as deeply as I loved him. I sat in his room, read the things he wrote, and listened to his music. I did everything I possibly could to stay connected to him. I couldn't get used to being without my son. Night after night, I begged God to let me dream about Joseph so I could hear his voice, look into his eyes, and embrace him one more time.

Going through the basic motions of each day was like rowing a boat through quicksand. It took everything I had and left me worn and weary. I looked at photos of him and remembered each moment—the day of his birth; his first walk with Daddy down a sidewalk and those little bare feet; watching cookies bake in the oven while all wrapped up in his green blanket; the first time his toes met the ocean and took his breath away; and then all grown up at the beach with his brothers, eating watermelon on the porch. Moments that once brought tears of happiness to my eyes did so again but this time as tears of pain. I didn't want to look at him in pictures. I wanted to look at him in life. Pictures became remnants of my happiness.

Grief didn't come with instructions. It was a crash course. I vaguely remember learning the stages of grief in Psychology 101. What I was completely unprepared for is that they come and go multiple times a day, sometimes an hour. They wreaked havoc on my mind and body. I thought you went through each step one by one, one nice neat step at a time, and then voilà—it was over. But I knew nothing.

Grief swallowed my brain the minute Joseph died. My memory turned to mush, and it threw my family and me for a loop. With Phil, Curt, and Wyatt the artists of the family, I was the heart of the home, keeper of the schedule, and the glue that held my very creative family together.

But I simply lost my memory. I could not even take a shower correctly. I would step in and take comfort in the warm water. I would step out and not remember if I shampooed my hair and would have to get back in. This happened over and over again. One morning, I found myself curled up on the bathroom floor, sobbing uncontrollably, convinced I was going crazy.

Week after week, I failed to show up for my appointments and failed to remind my men of theirs. Though never intentional, dental appointments were missed, haircut appointments overlooked, and planned get-togethers forgotten. My brain had become scrambled. It no longer helped to write things on a calendar, as I couldn't even remember to look at it. I was the organized one of the family, the one each of my men depended on. Therefore, we became a mess.

We did manage to make it to most functions having to do with Curt and Wyatt. We met with teachers and went to ballgames. I attribute that to having good friends on the teams and in the schools who gently reminded us. Quite honestly, that is all we could muster. I know now that that was okay. We cannot walk out of the cemetery and back into life as we knew it. We must take time to grieve.

People treat you differently after the funeral. I didn't like being the center of attention, yet it was painful when people pretended Joseph's death never happened or, worse, acted as though he *never existed*. Some people purposely turned another direction when they saw me at a distance in Walmart or at the ball field, not knowing what to say to the dead boy's mom. I found it easier to stay home.

Thankfully, there is humor in the midst of grieving, something that brings welcomed moments of relief from the pain, and we embraced those gifts from God. Being able to laugh kept me sane. Phil's job at the time required him to travel each week, and he was typically gone half the week. For the first three or four weeks after Joseph's death, he was able to work from home. The time came, however, when he had to get back on the road. I dreaded it.

Prior to leaving the ER that fateful day, the doctor gave both Phil and I a prescription for what I assume was an antianxiety medication. Although you'd never have been able to tell, Phil took it immediately and stayed on it for two or three days. But I hadn't taken any. The morning he left, however, I decided I would since it was the first day I'd be home to face the emptiness alone.

Phil left early, and Curt left shortly thereafter. While driving Wyatt to school, I told him he'd have to take the bus home that afternoon, as I was going to take medication and thought it best not to drive.

I was home for two or three hours when the school called. The lady on the phone informed me that Wyatt was having a rough day and wanted to come home. She proceeded to tell me, "Mrs. Ramsey, he said you're unable to pick him up … because you took drugs." She chuckled. "Mrs. Ramsey, I understand. With your permission, I'll bring him home myself." It was such a welcome relief to chuckle along with her.

One minute I would be fine, thinking to myself, *Okay, I can make it through this.* Then out of the blue, the grief would engulf me again. There seemed no rhyme or reason. The unexpected in the ordinary days caused tidal waves of grief for me without so much as a moment's notice.

Several months after Joseph died, I went grocery shopping and spotted his favorite Cream of Rice cereal placed where it had always been, on the top shelf, next to the Cream of Wheat. But this time, it caught me off guard. I burst into tears, remembering. I left my full cart in the aisle, ran out the door, jumped in my van, pressed my face into the steering wheel, and sobbed like a baby. Completely undone, I sat there in the Food Lion parking lot bawling uncontrollably, purging my grief. I missed my boy so badly that every cell in my body hurt. Anyone who has not walked this journey would not have understood. I doubt the bagboy who was collecting carts in the parking lot did, but that's okay. Those of us on the mourning bench must let ourselves be broken and allow ourselves to hurt.

Traveling to visit family and friends didn't happen for a very long time. The thought not only overwhelmed me but also disheartened me when I considered a family trip without my entire family. Once we did start traveling, it was as awkward for our hosts as it was for us. We were lost on a family trip with one-fifth of our family absent, and those hosting us clumsily danced around the issue of our missing piece. I found it less painful to stay home. And so I did—for years.

Joseph did not get to officially graduate from high school. He finished his courses but never walked through a graduation ceremony. I had begun planning but did not get to host his graduation party. I could not bring myself to attend any graduations until Curt graduated three years later. And that was okay. Likewise, the weddings of Joseph's friends were difficult and often skipped. We loved his friends dearly, but each wedding was another reminder of a daughter-in-law we would not have and grandchildren we would not spoil, and we grieved them, too. I did what I needed to do, and I recommend other parents do so as well.

Friend, your grief will not look the same as mine, but it will overtake you. Sometimes in ways you might expect, sometimes in ways you will never see coming. You may find comfort in visiting family and friends when I couldn't. You, too, may forget to show up to all kinds of appointments. You may fall apart in public on a day you don't expect. The important thing is that you recognize that your grief will manifest in different ways at different times and that you need to give yourself the time, space, and permission to let it happen.

CHAPTER

25

God Can Handle Our Anger

I see now that my faith was becoming an ally rather than an enemy because I could vent anger freely, even toward God, without fearing retribution.

—Gerald Sittser, *A Grace Disguised*

God can handle our anger. He will not reject us. He will accept and even use our anger. My husband was angry at God for a couple of months after Joseph died. He was angry that God took Joseph and angry that we were robbed of Joseph's future. But God did not rebuke Phil for being angry, and with work and over time, he moved through it.

I don't remember saying I was angry at God when Joseph died, but that doesn't mean I wasn't. I knew Joseph belonged to God and not me. I also never blamed a person for Joseph's death, as there was no one to blame. I was confused, however, that others went on living life when my world came to an abrupt halt. It was ugly.

One evening, I picked up the newspaper. I'm sure I was looking at the obituaries, as that's all the news I cared about at the time. There was an entire page of General District Court information. *Who cares how much one was fined for going 41/25? That's not newsworthy or important. My world has stopped. A treasured child is dead, and people are spending valuable time reading nonsense?* The thought of people spending time on the mundane really annoyed me. The realization that others had gone on with living life was equally upsetting. I whipped the paper across the room and soon thereafter canceled my subscription. Looking back, I don't know what I thought I was proving, but it was the only way I knew to be proactive, however wrong it might have been.

At the time of Joseph's death, I was the administrative assistant at our church. When I returned to work after his death, Joseph's name had been deleted from my computer. I am certain that was an act of love done for me so I would not have to be the one to remove his name from the software program. However, it was a reminder that with the press of a button my son no longer existed to others—his school, the college he chose to attend, and the scholarships he applied for. I thought about the legal, medical, and governmental offices his existence was deleted from and became enraged. With every ounce of my being I wanted to heave my office computer out the window, scream at the top of my lungs, and announce to the world that my son was still very real to me, that he could not just be deleted. Just the fact that "delete" buttons existed infuriated me!

An elderly friend depressed by the state of the world after one of the school shootings walked into my office and told me how lucky I was that Joseph was gone and didn't have to know such tragedy. I contemplated lunging across my desk and pulling every hair out of her head. I wasn't going to literally do it, but in my mind, she was as bald as an eagle. I was not "lucky" that Joseph was gone. I know my friend did not intend to upset me, but at that time, I was not in the frame of mind to distinguish her sadness from my pain.

The thing that angered me the most was people reminding me that "at least you have the other two"—as if I could pull them out of the trunk like a spare tire. Curt and Wyatt are not the substitutes. I love each of my three individually. They are not interchangeable. Even in grief, I was first and foremost a mama. You don't disturb a mama bear or meddle in her relationships with her cubs. Mama bears can be mean when protecting their young, and this one was no exception. If looks could have killed during that phase of my grief, I would now know fewer people.

I closed myself off from nearly everyone for a very long time. Other than my men, I felt disconnected from most people. I believe our relationships with others reflect our relationship with God. If that is true, my relationship with Him was in sad shape, as I remained withdrawn from nearly everyone for a good five to seven years.

I didn't want to meet new people. I didn't want to explain that my son recently died. I also didn't want to bring someone new into our life who didn't know Joseph and whom he never knew. New friends would have no reason to mention his name and would consider us a family of four. That was too upsetting to me.

Friend, are you angry? Do you want to scream at God? Go ahead. He can handle it. Go outside and scream at the top of your lungs. Say whatever you need to say. Cry as long and as hard as you want. Throw something if you need to. If I lived next door, I'd walk over and hold you up in the midst of your agony.

CHAPTER

26

Truth or Dare with God

No one ever told me that grief felt so like fear. I am not afraid, but the sensation is like being afraid. The same fluttering in the stomach, the same restlessness, the yawning. I keep on swallowing.

At other times, it feels like being mildly drunk, or concussed. There is a sort of invisible blanket between the world and me. I find it hard to take in what anyone says. Or perhaps, hard to want to take it in. It is so uninteresting. Yet I want the others to be about me. I dread the moments when the house is empty. If only they would talk to one another and not to me.

—C. S. Lewis, *A Grief Observed*

I was not overwhelmed by self-imposed guilt when Joseph died. I was not a perfect mom, but I knew I was a forgiven one. We were an affectionate family and very big on family meetings. We took time to clear the air, apologize, and forgive. "I love you" was verbalized and demonstrated regularly. Joseph died suddenly, yet I've never felt we left any part of our relationship unfinished.

I never went through the if onlys—*if only* he had a different car . . . , *if only* he had stayed home that morning . . . , *if only* I'd been a better person . . . , etc. My faith taught me that there is a time to live and a time to die. I firmly believe that February 23, 2002 was the day God chose to take Joseph home even before he was born. I accept that—but I hate it.

I knew I couldn't return to life as I knew it before Joseph died, so I never asked God to wake me from what was surely a nightmare. I did worse! I attempted a game of Truth or Dare with God. I begged Him to show this world just how big and powerful He really is. As I lay in my bed unable to sleep I challenged Him. *Pull out another miracle. Send him back. You can do that. You're God.* In my mind, I envisioned how utterly fantastic it would be for others to see what a mighty and awesome God we serve. They could witness a modern-day miracle! I was convinced the only way for this to happen was for God to send Joseph back. It would be a win/win situation! Dozens would come to know Jesus—and I'd have Joseph home in time for supper.

I was so desperate to see my boy that it didn't occur to me how selfish it was to ask to have Joseph leave the presence of the Father and come back to little ole Virginia. It also wasn't within my realm to realize that God really didn't need me to tell Him how to reveal Himself or what to do. I just knew I was in severe pain and having Joseph alive with me again would make my pain disappear. And so I dared God to prove Himself.

CHAPTER
27
Everything Looked Gray

Part of every misery is, so to speak, the misery's shadow or reflection: the fact that you don't merely suffer but have to keep on thinking about the fact that you suffer. I not only live each endless day in grief, but live each day thinking about living each day in grief.

—C. S. Lewis, *A Grief Observed*

Joseph died on February 23. By the first of March, family and friends had gone home and back to work. But I had not. My world stopped. Life was a merry-go-round, traveling one hundred miles per hour. I didn't fall off; I was kicked off. I woke each morning and found myself lying face down in the dirt, choking. Every bone felt broken, and liquid heartbreak oozed from every pore. It was dizzying and maddening to watch others securely fastened to the merry-go-round, traveling at such a fast rate of speed.

Grief aged me at least ten years, probably fifteen, in a split-second. One morning I was a happy, thirty-nine-year-old woman, and the next minute, I barely recognized the worn-down, defeated woman in the mirror.

Once the arrangements were made, the funeral over, and everyone gone, color disappeared from my world. Everything and everyone looked gray. Even my tears looked gray. My purpose in life was lost, and my energy was nearly nonexistent. I didn't care about my health. Vitamins were disposed of, exercise stopped, and doctor's appointments canceled. A terminal prognosis would have been welcomed. Grief affected every ounce of my being and each of my senses and robbed me of the desire to live. It inhabited my brain and turned my mind to mush. Sleep was my only relief. It was the only time the trauma wasn't gnawing at me.

Before Joseph died, I read books regularly. After he died, I was not able to focus and read the same pages over and over. My concentration was sporadic at best, and that only added to my frustration. I thought back to grammar school when we had to read a paragraph and then fill in the blanks about what we'd just read. I would have failed grammar school the year my son died.

I used to pride myself at work for being a conscientious and diligent worker, always willing to learn new tasks. So much for pride! That was the first thing to fly out the window when I buried my child. I returned to work two weeks after Joseph died. I lasted an hour. I returned home and stayed there another two weeks. Once back, I did my very best, but it wasn't very good. No one complained, but I knew. I had to keep a to-do list on my desk so I wouldn't forget what had to be done which day. I wrote step-by-step instructions for myself how to do everything I was responsible for and had known how to do for years. Everything had to be written down and then crossed off once completed. It was the only way I could keep track.

Wyatt's birthday was a few weeks after Joseph died. I used to love making birthdays special for each of my boys. There was always a fun birthday tablecloth, plates, and napkins. The cake was made from scratch or ordered from a bakery, decorated with that birthday's theme, and placed in the center of the table. A bouquet of balloons floated from the birthday boy's chair. Well-thought-out presents wrapped and tied with a ribbon stood behind the cake, and the recipient's favorite snacks were intermingled. Pictures of past birthdays also adorned the table. But that year, nothing was planned. Thankfully, my sister was visiting, so I tossed a box cake mix into her hands, and she went into my kitchen and whipped up a party. Wyatt had asked for a new bike, so I called a friend down the street and gave her a blank check to get one. I did nothing—which was exactly all I was capable of doing.

By the time the auction was over in June, there were periods of time when a good day for me was waking up and actually crawling out from under the covers. A really good day meant I also showered. On a truly successful day, I made my family toast for breakfast. For the rest of that summer, I went to work at my part-time job and then came home at 1:00 and crawled into Joseph's bed and cried the afternoon away. Were it not for fast food my other two boys would have starved. By the end of the summer, I began withdrawing from people. I canceled everything I possibly could and often left Phil to attend his functions alone. I was depleted, an empty vessel; I had nothing to give. People thought I should have been over the worst, but I was actually in the throes of it.

A friend, trying to encourage me, told me to be patient with myself and allow at least one year to get through the worst. While very true, his advice and encouragement devastated me. I couldn't imagine living in that state an entire year. I was just trying to survive until lunch. Once lunch was over, I tried to survive until bedtime. Thinking long-term meant hanging on until the milk expired.

Summer came and went. The leaves began to change and let go, but my grief clung harder.

One fall morning after crawling out of bed to get my boys off to school and myself ready for work, I heard a knock at my bedroom door. Curt poked in his head. "Mama, sorry to bother you, but we don't have any clean jeans to wear to school." I told him "Sorry, honey. Please go to the laundry room and find your cleanest dirty jeans." Now I was forgetting to do the laundry. The truth is, I was doing hardly anything. And yet I was doing everything I possibly could. It's just that what was possible was very little.

That same month, Phil needed to be out of town for a few nights. One night, Wyatt was sitting at the dining room table, completing his homework. "Mama, I need help with math, please." He may as well have been asking me to help perform brain surgery. I tried to explain that I just wasn't able and encouraged him to call a friend. By the end of our conversation, we were both in tears. Curt, my math whiz, was at football practice, so he could not help. And once he did get home, he would have had his own homework to do. I simply did not have the wherewithal to help my child. Me, the one who my men counted on to keep things running smoothly! It would not have mattered if it were first-grade math. Finally, I called our friend Kevin and asked if he would help my youngest. He agreed, and he and his wife brought pizza for dinner. Dinner. I hadn't even thought about it.

But even during the worst of the grief, God gifted me with moments of laughter. Wyatt desperately wanted a dog. We were advised that pet therapy is a wonderful aid in grief recovery. At that point, I would have purchased a pet gorilla had I been told it would put smiles on my boys' faces again.

I called a local vet and asked for a breed recommendation. I explained that I wanted a healthy breed, not one prone to disease or illness. My boys didn't need anything else jerked out of their lives. Furthermore, I wanted one that would be okay for allergy sufferers. My preferences, too, were that it be a breed easy to train and one that likes to cuddle. And I absolutely did *not* want one that would shed. My lengthy must-have list continued. Finally, the vet said, "Mrs. Ramsey, I think you need a stuffed animal."

We ended up buying a miniature schnauzer for Christmas, and we each instantly fell in love with her.

Family and friends offered well-meaning words, but they seemed trite and hollow compared to the magnitude of my loss. Words did not console. When my grief was at its worst, time didn't heal, and being reminded of hope beyond the grave brought no comfort. I was incapable of handling anything, so telling me the Lord didn't give me more than I could handle was a waste of words. Someone suggested I take all the love I had for Joseph and spread it evenly between Curt and Wyatt. Really? Was I supposed to make that love dissipate as though it never existed? Pretend I never knew him? The love for the one I carried in my womb, birthed, nursed, raised, loved, and would have happily died for? His departure left a hole in my heart, a hole that is shaped like him. No one else can fit. I miss Joseph, who is an irreplaceable person. He had a name, a room in my home, a seat at my table, and a toothbrush at my sink.

CHAPTER
28
No Consoling Words

Talk to me about the truth of religion and I'll gladly listen. Talk to me about the duty of religion and I'll listen submissively. But don't come talking to me about the consolations of religion or I shall suspect that you don't understand.

—C. S. Lewis, *A Grief Observed*

Many people tried comforting us with words. But there are no consoling words! I really just wanted people to be quiet. I appreciated those who cried with me, hugged me, and offered a brief prayer, but words were unnecessary. I remember offering platitudes to others who were grieving before Joseph died. I no longer do. I know now that words cannot heal a broken heart.

When a friend loses a child, I no longer offer the following comments. Here are my personal explanations for each:

"Time heals"—Healing takes time, but time does not heal. A mother never ceases mourning the death of her child. Grief, like addiction, is always a part of us. We work through the process but remain in grief recovery.

"At least Joseph is in a better place"—My faith and intellect knew that, but I wanted him with me. I had not finished mothering him; he had not even left home. My family puzzle was missing a piece. Reminding me of hope beyond the grave brought no comfort.

"The Lord won't give you more than you can handle"—Intellectually, I knew that was true. But I wanted to die. I did not think I knew how to handle anything. Nothing. The death of my son challenged my faith.

"Joseph would want you to . . ." or "Joseph would not want you to . . ."—I didn't live my life to please Joseph before he died. I wasn't going to do so after he died.

"Be strong"—Those of us mourning are real people, and we need to acknowledge the magnitude of our loss. We are not rocks or robots. Ignoring our grief is not strength.

"I know how you feel"—No, you don't. No one will fully understand my loss. Burying a favorite aunt or pet, while heartbreaking, does not qualify you to know how a mama feels after burying a child. As difficult as it is, we know to expect to one day bury our grandparents, parents, and spouse. But we do not expect a child to die before us. Furthermore, each person's grief is unique.

"Let me know if I can do anything for you"—Creating things for people to do was exhausting. The many that noticed a need and met it were helpful. Grieving parents are not going to call and tell you what they need.

"At least you have the other two"—My boys are not interchangeable. I'm a mama of three. Having the other two does not make up for the absence of Joseph. All four of us miss Joseph, a wonderful young man who had a God-given personality, strengths, weaknesses, and a specific role in our family.

"He is a flower in God's garden"—Oh, my goodness. The dead do not become flowers, butterflies, raindrops, or even angels.

CHAPTER

29

With a Little Help from My Friends

Ah. I smiled. I'm not really here to keep you from freaking out. I'm here to be with you while you freak out, or grieve or laugh or suffer or sing. It is a ministry of presence. It is showing up with a loving heart.

—Kate Braestrup, *Here If You Need Me*

The first five years after Joseph died were agonizingly long. Time ceased to pass. My grief continued to ebb and flow. Some days went okay, and other days the grief reared its ugly head and wreaked emotional havoc. I continued to stay withdrawn although not reclusive. I attended the basics somewhat regularly—church, work, and my boys' school and sporting events—but did so with little zeal. I did what I had to do and nothing more. I pulled that off fairly well but then came home and collapsed. Social functions were avoided as much as possible, as it was draining to connect with people I otherwise wouldn't have. Most of my friends understood or at least dealt with it, and I didn't have the emotional energy to care what acquaintances or strangers thought.

My long-term friendships stood the test of time and grief. They were built on much more than commonalities. They were built on faith, commitment, and loyalty. I've never been one to have to chat with girlfriends on the phone daily so that was never expected. My friends did, however, find ways to reel me back in when they felt I was drifting too far away.

One of the most healing things were those closest to me listening as I talked about my memories of Joseph. My long-time and very dear friend Karen invited me to her home one day, and the two of us sat by her pool and talked, cried, and laughed for hours. What a ministry the gift of time and tears is to a grieving mom!

The ladies I prayed with regularly expected nothing from me as I sat with them in complete silence for months during our weekly time of prayer. They let me take my time to work my way back into praying with them. They held my hand and cried with me when I cried. What a blessing! I have no doubt my lovely friends prayed me through every step of my grief.

For months, another friend called me every time she heard the song "Arms Wide Open" on the radio to let me know she loved me. She saw my car pull into the cemetery one afternoon and pulled in behind me because she suspected I just might need a hug.

Two others sent cards monthly for a year. I still have most of them, as the personal notes in each were just what I needed the moment I received them.

God uses our friends. They are gifts from Him, and He loves us through them. I have several who hung in there with me when I was ugly, withdrawn, rude, depressed, crying, and wanted to give up. Each one comforted me, confronted me, and confided in me. And I am rich.

Despite having my good friends, some things remained difficult for years. For the first few years after Joseph died, I didn't attend church on Mother's Day. It was just too difficult. The next few years, I didn't want my presence to make my friends or other moms uncomfortable with their celebrations.

Admittedly, I still get melancholy on Joseph's birthday. I remember how exuberant Phil and I were the day he was born. Just as I could not describe the love I had for him that very moment, I cannot describe the depth to which I continue to miss him. I find myself wondering what could have been even though I now know it wasn't meant to be. I am writing this paragraph a week before my eldest would be celebrating his twenty-ninth birthday, and I wonder what he would have looked like, what job he might have had, and whether or not he would have had a family. I know that was not meant to be, but erasing eighteen years' worth of hopes and dreams does not happen overnight—or in a decade.

Chapter

30

Use Your Tears

Your most effective ministry will most likely come out of your deepest hurts.

—Rick Warren, *The Purpose Driven Life*

Within three months of Joseph's death, Phil, an artist, began healing. He also began to paint again. He painted a 50" x 60" painting entitled, "Do You Have Hope?" The majority and center of the painting is a portrayal of the crucifixion. To the side of Christ is an image of Joseph, fully alive. He is alive now because of the immeasurable love of Jesus and the price He paid. In an upper corner are avenging angels. Michael the archangel is holding the others back, keeping them from rushing to avenge the sacrifice of God. They never received that word.

This painting now hangs in the room that was once Joseph's bedroom. This room no longer contains his belongings, but the painting serves as a reminder that he is indeed alive and we do have hope. With his large painting set on an easel, Phil spoke to every youth group, church, and civic organization that would have him. He needed to offer others the hope that Joseph knew. Determined, Phil found purpose and began painting with more passion and vivid color.

It took me longer. My faith and mind told me I was here for a reason, but my body and will struggled. I wanted there to be a new book in the

Bible, 1 Shelley, containing one chapter for each day of my life, spelling out my purpose with instructions, preferably in three convenient steps. But that didn't happen. I had to work. I had to be intentional.

When I finally started working my way through the grief, I found purpose in mothering my younger sons and taking care of my home. As each left for college, a portion of my purpose left with him. I served no higher calling than to be a mama. Nothing brought me more joy; nothing came more natural.

My faith was challenged again in 2007. I was at work one morning when I learned gunshots were fired on the campus of Virginia Tech. Curt had transferred there the previous fall and was on campus and in class the day of the April 16 shootings. Once he was able, Curt called his dad to let him know he was okay and in lockdown in a classroom. Phil then called me at work to let me know.

I excused myself and went to the ladies room. I closed the stall door, dropped to my knees, thanked God, and wailed like a baby. I anxiously awaited Curt's next call, informing us that he made it safely to his car and back to his apartment, and then wept with joy when I heard his voice. This was yet another harsh reminder of the fragility of life. It was also a reminder that I am not exempt from losing another son. God's plan remains a mystery.

Every April when memorials of those lost during that tragic shooting air on TV, I pause again and thank God for Curt. My middle son has brought tremendous joy to our family. There is never a dull moment when he is around. I am humbled at the ways God is using him to enrich the lives of others and am delighted that he is using his God-given talent as an artist. I am immeasurably proud of the strong and courageous man that he is.

After several years, I finally arrived at knowing I couldn't stay where I was. I knew Jesus. I knew Joseph was home. I knew this earthly home was temporary. However, I realized what I hadn't done was surrender my grief to God. I had to go before Him and admit that He knew what was best and that I did not. I woke up those subsequent mornings and asked Him *each and every day* what He needed from me. One day at a time was all He required.

It took me a very long time to grieve, but I did eventually start reaching out to others. My prayer is that it won't take you nearly as long.

If you've buried a child or another loved one, give yourself ample time to grieve. Feel it, own it, and get it out. Then reach out to others. I had to start small. One fall, I made it a point to call and check in on friends who had children leaving for college. I put it on my calendar to call one friend or family member per week. A year or two later, I bought enough note cards and stamps to write one note a week for a year and then made myself do so every Thursday. I put it on my calendar and then checked it off my list.

Once you've taken ample time to grieve, reach out. Start, and do not stop.

Let's allow God to use our tears. Let's plant them and watch them grow as we become the ones who minister, the anonymous friends. The love and comfort God has given us is not only His ministry to us; it is His call to us to minister to others. Please, friend, do not waste as much time as I did.

CHAPTER

31

Trust God in the Dark

I am so weak. I can't read my Bible. I can't even pray. I can only lie still in God's arms like a little child and trust.

—J. Hudson Taylor, *Streams in the Desert*

Once I surrendered my grief, years' worth of depression started lifting and my mind started functioning better. I knew I had to be deliberate about taking steps out of the dark tunnel of grief. I had reached a crossroads. I had heard it said that grief makes you better or bitter. I had to decide which path I would take.

For several decades, I said I believed in God the Father, God the Son, and God the Holy Spirit and had put my confidence in Him. The hot crucible of grief was my place to back up what I said I believed and admit to myself who my God really was: The God I claimed to know, or a false god who can be manipulated into resolving the external circumstances of my life?

I began praying for the health and safety of my boys before each one was born. Once a week for two years prior to Joseph's death, I also gathered with other moms to pray for my sons and their schools, and I specifically asked God to protect the health and safety of Joseph, Curt, and Wyatt. My prayers were not answered the way I had hoped. Despite countless prayers for Joseph to be safe, God said no. His plan remains a mystery. I have had to accept that mystery and trust Him in the dark. I have had to trust His sovereignty, His love for me, and His ability. This meant stepping outside of myself and stepping inside the mystery of Jesus. Everything about that goes against my nature. Yet it was the most essential part of growth for me. I was not, however, able to do this before I allowed myself to fully grieve Joseph. The only way out of grief is to work through it. Working through grief is imperative and is the only portal to Christ when this kind of tragedy befalls us.

I wish I could tell you that there are three easy steps and, once completed, everything will be wonderful. But that's not how it works. We can, however, know peace and joy at a level we've never known before. We can experience oneness with God that we may not have otherwise. It took me years, but I have that oneness now and really want you to have it too.

I was in such bad shape that I had to begin with the most basic. I made a short to-do list for myself every day: (1) Get up and dress for work. (2) Make a plan for dinner. (3) Throw in a load of laundry. (4) Touch base with someone today. Yes, grief hit so hard I had to start at the beginning. And knowing what I know now, I would also add: (5) Jot down one thing I am thankful for.

Other things I found necessary to progress the journey were journaling, worship, and prayer. Once I worked through the long and arduous process of each of these, I was finally able to choose joy. Descriptions for each are detailed in the sections that follow.

CHAPTER

32

Journaling God's Faithfulness

God of our life, there are days when the burdens we carry chafe our shoulders and weigh us down; when the road seems dreary and endless, the skies grey and threatening; when our lives have no music in them, and our hearts are lonely, and our souls have lost their courage. Flood the path with light, run our eyes to where the skies are full of promise; tune our hearts to brave music; give us the sense of comradeship with heroes and saints of every age; and so quicken our spirits that we may be able to encourage the souls of all who journey with us on the road of life, to Your honour and glory.

—Augustine, *Works and Biography*

A friend of Phil's advised that we keep journals. He lost a son one year prior and knew well the importance journaling plays in grief recovery. Culture's demands are overwhelming for someone just beginning this journey. We are expected to return to work or school and resume the mantle of everyday life much too soon. Women are given an entire year for maternity leave in other countries, but we take a meager few days off when a child dies. Journaling affords us a much-needed outlet. It is a way to cry out to God in the midst of our grief and gives us an opportunity to express what we prefer not to share with others or what we think others cannot handle.

There is no right or wrong in journaling. You write when you want to about what you need to. You can express every thought, every emotion, and use whatever language your heart desires.

After my son died, I started a journal and then tossed my thoughts in the trash. A few months later, I tried again. I did that several times. My husband wrote fairly regularly for three years, every emotion raw. He was able to wallow there and write with brutal honesty and thus avoided taking the ugliness out on people. I wish I had kept all of my writings as opposed to being ashamed of them.

Phil and I wrote about our dreams of Joseph. We penned our favorite memories of him and our laments when the pain seemed unbearable and God felt very distant. We could say things in journals that people would have found irreverent. God didn't care nor did He leave.

Journaling is a written testimony to God's faithfulness and the ways He chooses to mature us. I made it about me. I feared someone would come across my writings one day and see what a mess I truly was. I was wrong. By discarding my early journals, I missed the opportunity to record God's working.

I had not read Phil's journal until preparing for this book. Actually, he hadn't either. Indeed it is a marvelous testimony to God's faithfulness. We read those pages and saw firsthand how far He has brought us along this painful and unwanted journey.

Journaling now offers me hope as I see His workmanship, His promises that He kept, and His unconditional love poured into me. You can know this too.

CHAPTER

33

Worship in Spite of Grief

The deepest level of worship is praising God in spite of pain, trusting Him during a trial, surrendering while suffering, and loving Him when He seems distant.

—Rick Warren, *The Purpose Driven Life*

Worship is showing adoration and honor to God; it is what we were created for. Worship is an invitation given only to those created in His image, human beings. It is our response to Him for who He is and what He has done. I love Ann Voskamp's thoughts on worship, "Every moment I live, I live bowed to something. And if I don't see God, I'll bow down before something else."[1] While tempting at moments, bowing down to grief and bitterness was not a choice I was willing to make.

I continued to worship in the days, months, and years following Joseph's death. Worship was an integral part of my grief recovery. I knew my soul needed to be fed. Although my active participation was minimal for a while, the Word of God was soaking into my head and nourishing my heart. It forced me take my eyes off myself and focus on Him. I worshipped in spite of my grief, never in place of it. I found my most profound experiences of worship were after the death of my son. The purpose for Christ's birth, death, and resurrection became so real I could taste it.

I needed to meet with God. I needed to know Him more intimately. I wanted to love Him more, to become more like Him. That is my prayer every morning. That is what I pray for my husband, sons, and daughter-in-law. He didn't fill the hole in my heart where Joseph lived; He is my heartbeat.

Before Joseph's death, I sang songs and hymns and enjoyed them. Since his death, I sing them with passion and empathy. "It Is Well With My Soul"[2] took on new meaning, and "I Need Thee Every Hour"[3] became an anthem. Before his death, I read and memorized Scripture, but since his death, all Scripture reads differently. It now pierces my soul, has become more applicable. I relied heavily on the little bit of Scripture I had memorized to get me through the darkest days. God matured me for His good, albeit painfully. All Scripture reads differently from this side of life. Job has become a personal friend.

It slowly sank in . . . eternity starts now and continues through death.

34

Coming Before Our Father

Prayer does change things, all kinds of things. But the most important thing it changes is us. As we engage in this communion with God more deeply and come to know the One with whom we are speaking more intimately, that growing knowledge of God reveals to us all the more brilliantly who we are and our need to change in conformity to Him. Prayer changes us profoundly.

—R. C. Sproul, *The Prayer of the Lord*

At the height of my grief, I was clueless as to how to do anything, including pray. Jesus knew there would be times we'd need help coming before the Father, so he gave us an illustration in the Lord's Prayer. This is the way Jesus taught His disciples to pray. Reciting this prayer one line at a time, very slowly, helped me through many long nights. Singing it did too.

> Our Father which art in heaven,
> Hallowed be thy name.
> Thy kingdom come
> Thy will be done in earth,
> as it is in heaven.
> Give us this day our daily bread.
> And forgive us our debts

as we forgive our debtors.

And lead us not into temptation

but deliver us from evil

For thine is the kingdom, and the power, and the glory,

for ever. Amen.

—Matthew 6:9-13 KJV

I relied on the following pattern as I attempted to renew my time with the Lord—praise, confession, thanksgiving, and intercession. I had been praying this way for a few years with other moms and knew it well.

I *praise* God by expressing words of honor to Him for His name, His character, and His Word. Even in the midst of mourning, He is worthy of praise. I wasn't able to praise Him at first, and He was fine with that. He knew I was suffering, and He understood. He is a big God, and He waited patiently and lovingly until I was ready.

Coming before God and *confessing sin* is cleansing. He is always ready to forgive my doubts and failures.

Giving thanks in everything is not something I wanted to do right after burying my son. That was okay with God too. In time and with practice, it became more natural.

Friend, are you stuck? Heading toward bitterness? Thank Him for the little things. Were you able to get up and get dressed today? After all you've been through, that's something to be thankful for! Are you doing better than you were a week ago? Thank Him. Did God love you through someone today? Thank Him. Have you been able to smile for even one second this week? Wonderful! Thank Him.

Years after Joseph died, I read *One Thousand Gifts* by Ann Voskamp.[1] At her recommendation, and thanks to her example, I began recording His graces each day, at least three a day. I found there are so many things to be thankful for. In doing so, thanks became the pulse of my prayer and my time with Him as opposed to giving Him a to-do list. That part of my journal causes me to focus on what He has done and what He is doing and helps take my focus off my grief.

Intercession is the privilege of coming before God on behalf of others. When I first began this journey of grief, the only people I was capable of praying for were my husband and sons. It took months before I was able to pray for others, and God understood.

I live near a hospital and a short distance from the helipad. When I heard the siren of an ambulance or the whirl of the helicopter in those first months of praying, I prayed for the one injured and his or her parents. After that, I included the state troopers, EMTs, and the firemen—those who deal with these horrendous deaths day in and day out. Little by little, other people were added. Intercession.

My experience is that God will meet us *anywhere*. Grieving badly and under the covers? He's there. Sitting at the cemetery, wishing it were you? You're not alone. Sitting on your child's bedroom floor still in your nightgown in the middle of the afternoon? He's holding you up. God will meet you *anywhere*. He *is* in the details. He was with me when I was in the bathroom throwing up because grief turned my stomach inside out. He was with me in the Food Lion parking lot when I sobbed so hard I couldn't catch my breath. And He was with me on the bathroom floor when I thought I was losing my mind. He's always been there. He's always available. When I needed peace the most, He scooped me up in His arms, kissed me on the forehead, and gave me rest. Friend, that's what He wants to do for you too.

I know you are hurting. God knows much better than I do. Pray. Lean into Him, and pour your heart out to Him. He's listening. He knows your name and sees each tear that falls. He understands your darkest moments and sorrows. He will enter each with unrelenting love and amazing grace.

CHAPTER
35
God Has Overcome the World

Joy is based on the spiritual knowledge that, while the world in which we live is shrouded in darkness, God has overcome the world.

—Henri Nouwen, *Here and Now*

Joy is true contentment that comes from internal factors like our faith in the Lord. It is not dependent on our circumstances, whereas happiness is. Nothing about the death of my son has made me happy, yet I have come to know true joy.

It was imperative for me to sit on the mourning bench for a period of time after burying Joseph. When new to the grief process, I was certainly not ready to choose joy. As I slowly put one foot in front of the other and walked this unwanted journey, I eventually reached a fork in the road. At that fork, I had to choose the path of joy or the path of bitterness. I chose joy.

Even though we've tasted death, we can know deep joy if our confidence is in the Lord whose joy is our strength (Nehemiah 8:10). We will continue to miss our children. That is as it should be. But be joyful. We can have a peace that passes all understanding at a time it makes no sense to know peace (Philippians 4:7). Celebrate life. Celebrate by being thankful. Thank Abba for moments of peace and moments of laughter. In the midst of grief, they are gifts from Him. Then thank Him when those moments turn to hours, days, and weeks of peace. Be joyful because He *will* use our suffering. Be joyful that the land of no more good-byes is in our future.

We cannot waste our pain. We cannot waste our tears. We must plant them and let them grow. Let's choose joy. Let's reach for the gifts God gives. Let's thank Him for each and watch joy grow. Each of us is created in the image of God. Let's be joyful! We're being sustained by the God of all grace. Let's be joyful! God has overcome the world. Let's be joyful! He has overcome death. Let's be joyful!

"Joy does not simply happen to us. We have to choose joy and keep choosing it every day."[1] As that is so true for me, I have "Choose Joy" as my computer screensaver. I need to remind myself of it every day.

God puts His reputation in our hands. We are privileged with the opportunity of allowing Him to be glorified in our suffering.

Chapter

36

One Who Treads for Us

Gifts of grace come to all of us. But we must be ready to see and willing to receive these gifts. It will require a kind of sacrifice, the sacrifice of believing that, however painful our losses, life can still be good—good in a different way than before, but nevertheless good. I will never recover from my loss and I will never get over missing the ones I lost. But I still cherish life. I will always want the ones I lost back again. I long for them with all my soul. But I still celebrate the life I have found because they are gone. I have lost, but I have also gained. I lost the world I loved, but I gained a deeper awareness of grace. That grace has enabled me to clarify my purpose in life and rediscover the wonder of the present moment.

—Gerald Lawson Sittser, *A Grace Disguised*

Grief ebbs and flows like the ocean tide. Some waves rise to engulf us and suck us into the undercurrent. Others cause us to merely lose our footing and throw us off balance. In the first years after Joseph's death, there were many life-threatening tidal waves that knocked me over and left me gasping for air. There seemed no rhyme or reason as to how each would hit, and their timing was completely unpredictable.

When tossed about by the waves of sorrow, we're submerged in disorienting darkness. When I was thrust into those deep waters, God was with me, and He remains there with me. I have come to understand that the serene shore of safety is an illusion. Life is turbulent, and we are all desperate for assistance. In my desperation, I realized that I did not have the energy or ability to fight the current that was drowning me. So I succumbed to the sorrow crashing around me.

Trying to fight the waves is an exercise in futility. Their consistent sting was a constant reminder of the reality of death, and there was nothing I could do to overcome it. I still have no control over the rising emotions that rush at me from the memories of my son. Nothing on this earth is permanent. It is all passing sand into uncharted water. This is a reality that I have learned to embrace. I am helpless to the whims of the waves. You are too.

But we find our hope in the one who treads for us, who refuses to let us get swallowed up by the tides of grief if we will only grab onto Him. He is as real as the crashing pangs of loved ones gone. And when we are helpless and lost without a foot on anything solid, He meets us there and accomplishes what we cannot. He is our lifeboat, keeping us afloat.

Afterword

Joseph's home-going was over eleven years ago. My wounds are no longer raw, but they are not gone. Giving God thanks is salve for them. The more I thank Him, the more they heal. Neglecting thanks exposes their rawness.

As I've learned to give thanks along this journey, I have opened a window and made a place for God to mature me. He is using the death of my son to refine my faith.

We are not here to just go through the motions of each day. God has given each of us a purpose. Those of us on the mourning bench must give ourselves ample time to grieve. That is imperative. God will then use our grief once we've surrendered it to Him.

I've learned slowly and have made many mistakes. Friend, my prayer is that you will be much quicker at learning to give thanks, and that Christ will be exalted in your grief and in your life. I've bathed these most personal moments and most intimate details of my life in prayer, asking God to use them to shorten your unwanted journey.

I understand that in the midst of grief some hours feel like years. Realistically, life on this earth is short. Press on. Don't lose hope. Keep your eyes on heaven. Eternity starts now. I hope you'll join me in choosing joy.

I wish we were sitting on my screened-in porch with an ice cold glass of lemonade or in my family room next to the fireplace, sipping hot chocolate, and could chat the afternoon away. I'd love to hear all about your loved one. In heaven, let's talk long.

Shelley

Scripture to Encourage You

"He tends his flock like a shepherd: He gathers the lambs in his arms and carries them close to his heart" (Isaiah 40:11 NIV).

"When you pass through the waters, I will be with you; and when you pass through the rivers, they will not sweep over you. When you walk through the fire, you will not be burned; the flames will not set you ablaze" (Isaiah 43:2 NIV).

"These things I have spoken to you, that in Me you may have peace. In the world you will have tribulation; but be of good cheer, I have overcome the world" (John 16:33 NKJV).

"Come to Me, all who are weary and heavy-laden, and I will give you rest" (Matthew 11: 28 NASB).

"Even though I walk through the valley of the shadow of death, I fear no evil, for You are with me; Your rod and staff, they comfort me" (Psalm 23:4 NASB).

"God is our refuge and strength, and ever-present help in trouble" (Psalm 46:1 NIV).

"Cast your burden on the Lord and He will sustain you" (Psalm 55:22 NASB).

"And He will wipe away every tear from their eyes; and there will no longer be any death; there will no longer be any mourning, or crying, or pain; the first things have passed away" (Revelation 21:4 NASB).

"Yet what we suffer now is nothing compared to the glory He will reveal to us later" (Romans 8:18 NLT).

Acknowledgments

To these, I humbly say, "Thank you":

The good people at WestBow Press with special thank-you to Mandy Tancak, Katherine Montgomery, Nate B., Mateo Palos, and Karol Canada: My goodness you all made the publication of this book a smooth process! Thank you for your promptness, professionalism, and guidance.

State troopers, EMTs, and firemen: God bless you for tirelessly and altruistically serving the public. Your work is of utmost importance and of tremendous value. Please know I come before the Father regularly on your behalf.

My anonymous friends: Living life with you has eased my sorrow, healed my grief, multiplied my joy, and taught me how to bear another's burdens. May you always serve so well as the hands and feet of the Savior as His arms continue to work through you.

My prayer partners: Your prayers and encouragement alone saw this project to fruition and allowed me to revisit this chapter of life only to exit stronger and more thankful. I know you have no need to see your names in print. I, however, need to publicly acknowledge that your friendship is grace at its purest.

Joy: For your time, expertise, and friendship I am indebted. That you would take time to re-enter this dark tunnel with me and pour over every thought, word, and punctuation mark is a gift. "Thank you" is inadequate but is offered with more love than thin letters can hold.

Michelle: I'm so glad Curt brought you into our lives. Thank you for gracing our family with beauty and joy. I am sorry Joseph did not live to know you. Of this I am certain: He would have loved and adored you as much as Phil, Wyatt, and I do.

Curt and Wyatt: I am honored to serve as your mama and graced to know you as brothers in Christ. You by far are the most captivating works of art I've ever encountered. Never forget that Jesus is writing a story on each of your lives and I am bathing those in prayer every single day.

Phil: Your walk with Christ has been a guiding light for me as we've traveled this unwanted journey hand-in-hand. Thank you for modeling through your tender leadership and strong example that eternity starts now. It has blessed me greatly and comforted me immeasurably to witness you become more like Jesus in the midst of your grief.

God the Father, God the Son, and God the Holy Spirit: I humbly thank You for drawing me close to You and never letting me forget that I always have been, am now, and always will be furiously and unconditionally loved. Indeed, I am homesick.

Notes

Heart Thought 8: No Coincidences

1. Mercy Me, "I Can Only Imagine," by Bart Millard, *Almost There*, ©2001 (INO/Curb).

Heart Thought 11: Arms Wide Open

1. Creed, "Arms Wide Open," by Scott Stapp, *Human Clay*, ©2000 (Wind Up Records).

Heart Thought 14: Buried on Hallowed Ground

1. Nicholas Wolterstorff, *Lament for a Son* (Grand Rapids, MI: Wm B Eerdmans, 1987), 100.

Heart Thought 33: Worship in Spite of Grief

1. Ann Voskamp, *One Thousand Gifts: A Dare to Live Fully Right Where You Are* (Grand Rapids, MI: Zondervan, 2010), 110.
2. Words by Horatio Spaford, Composed by Philip Bliss (1873) "It Is Well With My Soul."
3. Words by Annie S. Hawks, Composed by Robert Lowry (1872) "I Need Thee Every Hour."

Heart Thought 34: Coming Before Our Father

1. Ann Voskamp, *One Thousand Gifts: A Dare to Live Fully Right Where You Are* (Grand Rapids, MI: Zondervan, 2010).45.

Heart Thought 35: God Has Overcome the World

1. Henri Nouwen, quoted in *The Heart of Henri Nouwen*, Rebecca Laird and Michael J. Christensen, eds. (New York, NY: Crossroad, 2003).45.

Made in the USA
Lexington, KY
09 November 2013